The Unlisted Bible

OrangeBooks Publication

1st Floor, Rajhans Arcade, Mall Road, Kohka, Bhilai, Chhattisgarh 490020
Website: **www.orangebooks.in**

First Edition, 2025

ISBN: 978-93-7426-714-1

Price: Rs. 399.00

Printed in India

MASTER THE MINDSET, MECHANICS, AND STRATEGIES OF PRIVATE MARKETS

THE UNLISTED BIBLE

A BEGINNER'S GUIDE TO INVESTING IN PRIVATE COMPANIES

VINAYAK SAVANUR

OrangeBooks Publication
www.orangebooks.in

Dedication

For my parents and my wife — my pillars of strength, my constant encouragement, and the reason I had the courage to complete this journey.

Acknowledgments

Writing *The Unlisted Bible* has been as much a journey of reflection as it has been of research and experience. This book would not have been possible without the unwavering support, patience, and inspiration of many people who have shaped both my life and my understanding of investing.

To my **parents**, whose values of discipline, humility, and perseverance continue to guide me every single day—your belief in me has been the true foundation of my journey.

To my **wife**, whose encouragement and quiet strength gave me the confidence and balance to complete this work. Your support reminds me daily of the power of partnership and patience.

To my **mentors and teachers**, who nurtured my curiosity and taught me that financial wisdom is not about chasing wealth but about creating clarity.

To my **clients, colleagues, and readers**, whose trust and questions have continuously inspired me to think deeper and simplify the complex — you are the reason this book exists.

And to every **aspiring investor** who seeks to learn, grow, and act with understanding — this book is my small contribution to your journey. May it serve as a compass toward disciplined, purposeful, and lasting wealth.

Author's Note

Every generation witnesses its own investment revolution. In the 1980s, it was mutual funds. In the 2000s, it was equities. Today, it's the rise of private and pre-IPO investing — the quiet frontier where the next decade's wealth will be built.

But unlike public markets, this world has no ticker, no daily charts, and no media noise. It rewards patience, understanding, and informed conviction — qualities most investors are never taught. That's where *The Unlisted Bible* comes in.

I don't write from theory; I write from experience. As one of North Karnataka's pioneering Certified Financial Planners (CFP®) and SEBI Registered Investment Advisors, with 13+ years of real market exposure, I've guided over 100+ families toward financial clarity. Over the years, I've seen how investors chase trends and lose money — and how those who follow disciplined principles quietly build wealth over time.

This book is more than a guide to unlisted investing. It's a manual on how to think like an investor. It simplifies complex structures, explains valuation logic in plain language, and reminds us that success in finance depends as much on temperament as it does on numbers.

If you've ever wondered how early investors spot potential before IPOs, or why patience often outperforms timing, this book will give you both the tools and the mindset to find out. Read slowly. Reflect often. This is not a get-rich-quick guide — it's a long-term companion. And if you internalise even a few of its lessons, you'll never look at investing — or opportunity—the same way again.

— ***Vinayak Savanur***

Preface

Why This Book, Why Now?

If you are holding this book, chances are you've heard whispers about unlisted stocks. Maybe a colleague mentioned a hot pre-IPO opportunity. Maybe you saw a news headline about employees of a unicorn startup turning crorepatis overnight. Or maybe you simply felt the pull of something exciting — the chance to be "early" before the rest of the world catches on.

Welcome. You've stepped into one of the most fascinating — and misunderstood — corners of the investing universe.

The Rising Curiosity

For decades, unlisted shares were the domain of venture capitalists, private equity firms, and insiders with deep networks. Ordinary investors had little chance of participating.

But times have changed. New platforms, employee stock sales, and digital access have opened the gates. Suddenly, middle-class professionals, entrepreneurs, and small investors are exploring this once-hidden world.

And with that, curiosity is booming. People want to know:

- What exactly are unlisted stocks?
- How do you buy them?
- What are the risks and rewards?
- Can they really make me rich?

The Problem with Curiosity

Here's the danger: when curiosity meets limited knowledge, mistakes follow.

- Investors are lured by hype and buy at inflated valuations.
- They trust verbal promises instead of contracts.
- They put too much money in one flashy startup.
- They panic when liquidity vanishes and feel trapped.

For every success story you read in the headlines, there are dozens of silent failures. But you rarely hear about those.

This book exists to balance the story — to shine light where there is often only shadow.

Why This Book?

You don't need another textbook full of financial formulas. You don't need glossy startup propaganda. What you need is a **practical, honest, and patient guide** that takes you by the hand and says:

"Here's what unlisted investing really is. Here's how you can participate. Here's how you avoid disaster. And here's how you give yourself a fair shot at life-changing wealth — slowly, carefully, wisely."

That is what this book is.

What This Book Is (And Isn't)

- ❌It is **not** a get-rich-quick manual.
- ❌ It will **not** give you stock tips or insider shortcuts.
- ✅ It **is** a map through the jungle of private markets.
- ✅ It will give you checklists, stories, case studies, and playbooks.
- ✅It will prepare your *mindset* as much as your *wallet*.

Think of it as both a flashlight and a compass. It won't walk the path for you, but it will show you where the cliffs are — and where the trails to opportunity lie.

The Reader I Wrote This For

I wrote this for the beginner who feels overwhelmed. For the professional with ₹50,000 saved, wondering where to put it. For the curious aspirant who wants to invest early but doesn't want to be reckless.

If that's you, this book is your companion. It will teach you not just how to invest, but how to think like an investor — calm, patient, and disciplined.

A Final Thoughtbefore We Begin

The private market is exciting because it feels secretive, exclusive, full of promise. But remember:

> ***"Excitement is not a strategy. Patience is."***

If you carry nothing else from this book, carry this truth: **time is your greatest ally.**

Now, let's begin. Let's step into the jungle of unlisted stocks together — not with fear, not with greed, but with clarity, courage, and patience.

About the Author

Vinayak Savanur is a seasoned investor, educator, and financial professional with over **13 years of experience in the primary and secondary markets**. Holding a master's degree in finance, he made history as **North Karnataka's first Certified Financial Planner (CFP®)** and the region's **first SEBI Registered Investment Advisor (RIA)** — credentials that reflect both expertise and integrity.

Vinayak's journey began not with a single bold trade but with a simple curiosity: *why do most investors fail despite having access to the same markets?* That question led him to a career focused on education, ethics, and empowerment. Over the years, he has guided **more than 100 families secure their financial futures**, guiding them toward calm, disciplined, and sustainable investing — one decision at a time.

His insights have reached a wider audience as a **guest columnist for** Moneycontrol and through features in **Mint, Times of India, Deccan Herald, Vijayavani**, and The **Digvijay 24x7 News Channel**, where he is recognised for his ability to simplify complex financial concepts into practical, real-world guidance.

Today, through *The Unlisted Bible*, Vinayak continues his mission — to make the world of private and unlisted investing accessible, transparent, and intelligent for every aspiring investor.

> ***"Wealth isn't built by chance; it's shaped by patience, discipline, and understanding."***

Summaries

Part I: The Foundation

Chapter - 1: Why This Book?

Introduces the world of unlisted investing. Explains why ordinary investors are suddenly gaining access to a once-exclusive market, the allure and traps, and why patience and preparation are essential. Sets the tone that this is not a "get-rich-quick" manual but a long-term guide.

Chapter - 2: What Are Unlisted Stocks?

Defines unlisted stocks in simple terms. Explains the categories of: pre-IPO, startup equity, ESOPs, and mature private firms. Compares listed vs unlisted shares in terms of liquidity, transparency, regulation, and risk. Includes real-world examples and a beginner's toolkit.

Chapter - 3: The Allure of the Private Market

Explores why investors are drawn to unlisted shares: dreams of 100x returns, exclusivity, IPO excitement, and status. Balanced with cautionary tales (e.g., Byju's crash). Encourages readers to distinguish between story and substance.

Chapter - 4: The Risks and Realities

Details the darker side: illiquidity, lack of transparency, inflated valuations, scams, psychological traps, and regulatory blind spots. Uses case studies (Theranos, Paytm, Byju's) to highlight dangers. Provides a practical risk filter for beginners.

Part II: The Investor Mindset

Chapter - 5: Investor Psychology

Covers biases (FOMO, overconfidence, loss aversion, confirmation bias) that derail beginners. Explains how patience, scepticism, and resilience define successful investors. Includes an "Investor Journal" exercise.

Chapter - 6: Risk vs Reward

Explains the asymmetry of unlisted investing: potential for 100x returns but risk of total loss. Shows how professional investors think in probabilities and portfolios. Introduces a risk-reward matrix and reflection tools.

Chapter - 7: The Power of Long-Term Thinking

Demonstrates why holding for years (even decades) is key. Uses analogies like the bamboo tree and stories (Infosys millionaires, Flipkart exits). Encourages readers to resist the temptation of early exits.

Part - III: The Mechanics of Unlisted Investing

Chapter - 8: Where to Find Unlisted Stocks

Details the main sources: ESOP sales, brokers, online platforms, pre-IPO placements, private networks, and funds. Explains pros/cons, risks, and how to verify sources.

Chapter - 9: Understanding Valuations

Simplifies valuation methods: comparables, P/E, P/B, DCF, and last funding round price. Warns against hype-driven bubbles. Includes Byju's (failure) and IRCTC (success) as case studies.

Chapter - 10: Due Diligence Made Simple

Provides a beginner-friendly framework for financial, business, and management due diligence—lists red flags, tools (MCA, Crunchbase, Glassdoor), and layering approaches. Case studies include Theranos and smaller Indian startups.

Chapter - 11: The Legal Side

Explains critical documents (SHA, SPA, Demat, lock-ins), investor rights, and regulatory frameworks (SEBI, SEC). Warns against scams like fake certificates. Provides a legal checklist for protection.

Part - IV: Strategies & Playbooks

Chapter - 12: How to Start Small

Practical roadmap for first-time investors: start with ₹25–50k, focus on safer pre-IPO or ESOP deals, use trusted brokers, and treat initial investments as tuition. Includes a simple 3-year playbook.

Chapter - 13: Diversification in the Private Market

Shows why diversification is survival in unlisted investing. Explains dimensions: by stage, sector, ticket size, geography. Case study of a balanced portfolio that absorbed failures.

Chapter - 14: Exit Strategies

Outlines main exit routes: IPO, buybacks, acquisitions, secondary sales, PE exits. Explains timing traps, lock-ins, and how to plan before buying. Case studies include Flipkart, Paytm, and NSE.

Chapter - 15: Case Studies of Wins and Failures

Brings theory to life with real-world stories: Flipkart (win), IRCTC (win), Byju's (failure), Theranos (failure), Paytm (mixed). Extracts common patterns behind success and failure.

Part - V: Becoming a Mature Investor

Chapter - 16: Red Flags to Watch For

Protective toolkit of warning signs: overhyped valuations, guaranteed IPO promises, lack of transparency, shady founders, aggressive brokers, complex structures. Includes a 9-point red flag checklist.

Chapter - 17: Networking & Information Sources

Explains where serious investors find deals: brokers, angel networks, forums, events, and personal contacts. Covers reliable information sources (MCA, Crunchbase,

Glassdoor, news). Introduces the “3-Layer Rule” for verifying info.

Chapter - 18: Building Your Portfolio Over Time

Shows how to grow from small beginnings to a structured portfolio across 3 stages (foundation, expansion, maturity). Encourages tracking, rebalancing, and a farmer’s mindset.

Chapter - 19: The Future of Unlisted Investing

Explores trends: democratisation through platforms, tokenisation via blockchain, globalisation, stricter regulations, and the rise of AIFs/syndicates. Explains implications for small investors.

Conclusion

Chapter - 20: The Patient Investor

Ties everything together. Recaps lessons, re-emphasises patience and discipline, and provides a roadmap for the journey ahead. Encourages readers to water their “bamboo investments” and trust time as their greatest ally.

Table of Contents

Part - II
Investor Mindset

Part - III
The Mechanics of Unlisted Investing

Part - IV

Strategies & Playbooks

Part - V

Becoming a Mature Investor

Part - I

The Foundation

Chapter - 1

Why This Book?

The Secret behind Great Fortunes

Every generation has its own gold rush. In the 1800s, it was land and railroads. In the 1900s, it was oil and industrial companies. In the 2000s, it became a technology startup. But beneath all of these stories lies one timeless truth: **the people who made the greatest fortunes didn't wait until the opportunity was obvious to everyone — they got in early.**

Imagine being one of the first employees at Infosys in the early 1990s when the company offered stock to its staff at throwaway prices. Or consider an investor who picked up shares of Amazon during its private fundraising rounds before the IPO. Those shares, almost worthless at the time, turned into life-changing wealth over the next two decades.

We often hear these stories with awe. But rarely do we pause to ask:

"Why were ordinary people not part of these success stories?"

The answer is simple: **the gates to unlisted investing were closed.**

A Club for the Privileged Few

For most of financial history, investing in private companies was a privilege reserved for insiders: venture capital firms, private equity houses, and ultra-wealthy families.

If you were an average person — working a job, saving in fixed deposits, dabbling in mutual funds — the world of unlisted shares was invisible. You could buy shares of Infosys *after* it listed, but by then, the early 100x gains were already taken.

This was not by accident. Laws and regulations were designed to protect "unsophisticated" investors from risky private companies. While the intent was noble, it also meant that only the rich and connected could participate in the early stages of business growth.

The Gates Are Opening

Today, the landscape is shifting. Technology platforms, employee stock resale markets, and specialised brokers have made it possible for retail investors to access unlisted shares.

- **Employees selling ESOPs**: Startups like Flipkart and Paytm allowed early employees to sell some of their stock to outside investors before the IPO.
- **Pre-IPO brokers**: Firms now specialise in connecting small investors with opportunities in companies preparing to go public.

- **Digital platforms**: Online marketplaces aggregate private share sales, bringing them to a wider audience.

The once-secret club is no longer as exclusive. Ordinary investors can now get a seat at the table. But — and this is crucial — a seat at the table doesn't mean you're ready for the feast.

The Allure and the Trap

Let's be honest: the allure is powerful. Who doesn't want to say, "I invested in XYZ before it became a household name"?

But the unlisted world is not all fairy tales. For every Amazon, there are hundreds of failed dot-com startups. For every Infosys, dozens of IT companies shut down quietly. For every Flipkart success, there's a Byju's - style cautionary tale of valuations collapsing.

The trap lies in believing that **every unlisted stock is a lottery ticket to wealth.** It's not. Most are high-risk bets with uncertain outcomes.

📌 **Quick Example:**

A young professional in Bengaluru once bought unlisted shares of a promising startup at ₹500 per share, convinced it would soon list at double the price. Instead, the company ran out of cash within two years. The shares became worthless. He lost ₹2 lakhs — money he had saved for his first home.

The lesson? Opportunity and risk are twins. You cannot embrace one without acknowledging the other.

Why This Book Exists

If you are holding this book, you probably fall into one of three categories:

1. **The Curious Aspirant** – You've heard about unlisted shares and want to understand what the hype is about.
2. **The First-Time Investor** – You are tempted to make your first move, but don't know where to start or how much to risk.
3. **The Serious Learner** – You already invest in mutual funds, stocks, or real estate, and now you want to explore unlisted opportunities as a way to diversify.

This book is written for all three.

It is not a get-rich-quick manual. It will not teach you how to gamble. Instead, it is a **map of the territory** — a guide to the mountains, rivers, and pitfalls you'll encounter on your journey.

What You Will Learn

By the time you finish this book, you'll know how to:

- **Understand the landscape**: What unlisted stocks are, why they exist, and how they are different from listed ones.
- **Evaluate opportunities**: The basics of valuation, due diligence, and red flags.
- **Develop the right mindset**: Patience, discipline, and the long-term view.

- **Manage risks**: Avoiding scams, overexposure, and emotional mistakes.
- **Strategise wisely**: How to start small, diversify, and plan for exits.
- **Learn from history**: Case studies of spectacular wins and equally spectacular failures.

Think of this book as your personal mentor. Where others rush in blindly, you'll walk in prepared.

A Word of Caution

This book will often repeat one message in different forms: **do not mistake possibility for probability.**

Yes, it's *possible* you might invest in the next giant before it lists. But it's more *probable* that you'll face delays, disappointments, and sometimes losses. If you go in expecting quick riches, you'll likely end up burned.

But if you go in with the mindset of a patient gardener—planting seeds, nurturing them, and waiting for years—the odds tilt in your favour.

The Lottery Illusion

Many beginners treat unlisted investing like buying a lottery ticket. But here's the difference:

- A lottery is pure chance.
- Investing, even in risky startups, is partly skill.

Your ability to research, choose wisely, and control your emotions can turn what seems like gambling into a calculated risk. That's the journey this book will prepare you for.

A Beginner's Checklist Before You Read On

As you step into the world of unlisted shares, keep these questions in mind. They'll serve as your compass throughout the book:

1. Can I afford to lose the money I'm investing?
2. Am I prepared to hold for 5–10 years if necessary?
3. Do I know where this opportunity came from and why it exists?
4. Have I checked at least 2–3 sources before trusting information?
5. Am I diversifying, or putting all my savings into one dream?

If your answer to any of these is "no," don't worry. By the end of this book, you'll know how to say "yes" confidently.

Closing Thoughts: The Patient Investor

The unlisted market is like entering a jungle. It's beautiful, rich with resources, but also full of hidden dangers. Without a guide, you may lose your way. With preparation, you may not only survive — you may thrive.

This first chapter is your invitation. Ahead, we'll break down the world of unlisted investing into clear, understandable pieces. Each chapter will equip you with tools. By the time you finish, you won't just be wandering in the jungle — you'll know how to build a safe path.

So take a deep breath. The gates are opening. Step inside.

Chapter - 2

What Are Unlisted Stocks?

A Simple Starting Point

Imagine you walk into a fruit market. On one side, there are stalls selling apples and bananas with price boards — you can see what each costs, you can buy as many as you want, and you can walk away any time. That's like the **stock market** you're familiar with: listed companies on exchanges such as NSE, BSE, NASDAQ, or NYSE.

But then, you notice a small stall tucked away in the corner. It sells exotic fruits you've never seen before. There's no price board, no guarantee of supply tomorrow, and you can only buy if the seller agrees. Some fruits may be rare delicacies worth a fortune, while others may rot before you even taste them. That corner stall is the world of **unlisted stocks**.

The Official Definition

In simple terms:

"Unlisted stocks are shares of companies that are not listed on a formal stock exchange."

This means:

- They don't trade publicly.
- Their prices aren't quoted daily on market tickers.
- Buying and selling happen privately, often through brokers, employees, or direct deals.

They are sometimes called:

- **Private equity shares** (though technically, PE is an institutional version).
- **Pre-IPO shares** (if the company is preparing to go public).
- **ESOP shares** (when sold by employees).

Why Companies Stay Unlisted

You may wonder: if listing gives access to huge capital, why doesn't every company rush to go public? Here are the main reasons:

1. Stage of Growth

Startups and young businesses aren't ready for the strict reporting and compliance of stock exchanges. They prefer private capital.

2. Control

Founders often want to retain decision-making power without outside interference. Listing brings in regulators, analysts, and public scrutiny.

3. Costs of Listing

An IPO is expensive — investment banks, auditors, lawyers, and compliance costs can run into crores.

4. Strategic Choice

Some companies remain private for decades (like IKEA or Cargill) and still thrive. Others wait until valuations soar before listing.

Types of Unlisted Stocks

Not all unlisted shares are the same. Let's break them into categories you're most likely to encounter:

1. Pre-IPO Shares

- Companies close to going public often allow early investors to buy shares.
- Example: Before Paytm's IPO, pre-IPO shares were traded in private deals.
- Risk: IPO may get delayed or valuations may crash post-listing.

2. Startup Equity

- High-growth startups raise funds from angel investors, venture capitalists, or through ESOP sales.
- **Example:** Flipkart, in its early years, offered equity to investors before being acquired by Walmart.
- **Risk:** High failure rate — most startups don't survive beyond 5 years.

3. **Employee Stock Ownership Plans (ESOPs)**
   - Employees of private companies receive stock as part of their compensation. Sometimes they sell a portion before IPOs.
   - **Example:** Many early employees of Infosys and Wipro became millionaires through ESOPs.
   - **Risk:** Finding buyers and negotiating fair value is tricky.
4. **Private Placements by Established Companies**
   - Even mature companies sometimes remain unlisted for strategic reasons. Investors can buy shares through private deals.
   - **Example:** Reliance Retail was unlisted for years, and private investors who bought shares early saw significant value creation.

How Unlisted Stocks Differ from Listed Stocks

Aspect	Listed Stocks	Unlisted Stocks
Availability	Public exchanges (NSE, BSE, NYSE)	Private deals, brokers, employee sales
Liquidity	High – you can sell anytime	Low– selling may take months or years
Transparency	High – quarterly reports, disclosures	Limited – only basic financials available

Pricing	Market-driven, updated daily	Negotiated, no fixed price
Regulation	Strict (SEBI, SEC, etc.)	Light, often less oversight
Risk	Moderate	High (failure, illiquidity, fraud)
Reward Potential	Steady, compounding returns	Explosive, but uncertain

Real-World Examples

- **Infosys (1993)** – Investors who bought shares before its IPO saw 100x+ returns.
- **Flipkart (2007–2018)** – Early backers became wealthy when Walmart acquired it for $16 billion.
- **Byju's (2016–2023)** – Investors who bought unlisted shares at sky-high valuations saw the value collapse.
- **Theranos (2003–2018)** – A U.S. healthcare startup that raised billions privately but collapsed in scandal, leaving investors with nothing.

These examples illustrate the **dual nature** of unlisted investing: extraordinary upside, but brutal risks.

The Illusion of "Inside Information"

One of the dangers beginners face is being lured by so-called *exclusive tips*:

- "This company is about to go IPO, buy now!"
- "This startup is the next unicorn."

Here's the reality: if someone is offering you a "can't-miss" deal, chances are, professionals have already passed on it — or the risk is higher than you're being told. In unlisted markets, **information is power**, and you'll rarely have the full picture.

The Black Hole of Liquidity

In listed markets, if you regret buying a stock, you can sell it in seconds. In unlisted markets, you may be stuck for years. Liquidity — the ability to convert shares into cash — is the single biggest difference.

Think of it like real estate. You can't sell your house overnight just because you want to. Similarly, an unlisted share may have no buyer when you're ready to sell. Always remember: **money invested in unlisted shares should be money you can live without for years.**

Beginner's Toolkit: How to Identify an Unlisted Opportunity

Before you even think of investing, ask these five questions:

1. **What category is this share?** (Pre-IPO, ESOP, startup equity?)
2. **Why is it unlisted?** (Too young? Too secretive? Too expensive to list?)
3. **Who is selling to me?** (Employee, broker, founder?)
4. **How is the price being decided?** (Market comparable? Last funding round?)
5. **What's my exit plan?** (IPO, buyback, secondary sale?)

Closing Thoughts

At this stage, you should have one key takeaway: **unlisted stocks are not just "stocks you can't see on NSE or BSE." They are a parallel universe with their own rules.**

They can be doors to immense wealth — but also traps for the unwary. Understanding what they are, how they work, and why they exist is the first step to approaching them with wisdom.

In the next chapter, we'll look at the **allure of the private market** — why so many investors, despite the risks, are drawn to it like moths to a flame.

Chapter - 3
The Allure of the Private Market

The Dream Factor

Human beings are natural storytellers. We love the story of the underdog who rises against all odds — the garage startup that becomes a global giant.

When you hear that **Amazon began in Jeff Bezos's garage**, or that **Infosys was started with ₹10,000 borrowed from a wife's savings**, it stirs something in you. The thought creeps in:

"What if I could invest in the next one? What if I spotted the giant before the world did?"

This dream of finding the "next big thing" is the magnetic pull of the private market. It's the promise of being there early, before the crowd, before the media headlines, before the valuations skyrocket.

The Power of 100x

In the public market, we talk about **multibaggers** — a stock that grows 2x, 5x, or 10x. These are rare and celebrated. But in the unlisted world, stories of **100x or even 1000x returns** are whispered with awe.

- **Infosys**: Employees who held onto early shares saw their investments multiply by thousands of times over decades.
- **Flipkart**: Early investors who put in a few lakhs walked away with crores when Walmart bought it.
- **Zoom (USA)**: Investors in Zoom's private rounds saw astronomical gains after the company went public.

These stories create a sense of *fear of missing out (FOMO)*. You start to think:

"If they could do it, why not me?"

The Exclusivity Effect

There's also a psychological twist: **scarcity creates desire.**

Listed stocks are available to everyone, every day. But unlisted shares? They feel like hidden treasures — whispered about in investor circles, offered through exclusive networks, or shared by "those in the know."

Owning unlisted shares gives investors a sense of pride, of belonging to an inner circle. It feels like being a pioneer — someone who believed before the rest of the world caught on.

The IPO Temptation

The biggest allure is the **pre-IPO excitement.**

When a company announces its intention to list, the buzz begins. Brokers, employees, and early investors start trading shares privately, promising buyers that the IPO will bring huge gains.

This excitement feeds on two beliefs:

1. **IPO Premiums** – Many assume the listing price will always be higher than the pre-IPO purchase price.
2. **Liquidity Promise** – Once listed, you can sell easily and lock in gains.

Sometimes this belief works (Infosys, IRCTC). Other times, it crashes (Paytm, Zomato's post-listing slump). But the *dream of flipping pre-IPO shares for quick profit* continues to draw investors in.

The Emotional Hook

The private market doesn't just sell shares — it sells **dreams**.

- The dream of being part of something big.
- The dream of saying, "I was there before the world noticed."
- The dream of wealth that transforms not just your portfolio, but your identity.

It's no coincidence that many unlisted investment pitches sound more like stories than financial analyses. You don't just hear about revenue and profits; you hear about founders' vision, market disruption, and how this startup is going to "change the world."

Case Study 1: Flipkart's Fairy Tale

When Flipkart started in 2007, few imagined it would take on global giants. But early backers who put money into this online bookstore in Bengaluru saw their stakes grow beyond imagination.

In 2018, Walmart acquired Flipkart for $16 billion. Some early employees who had stock options suddenly became crorepatis. Early investors saw exits that turned lakhs into hundreds of crores.

This story became legendary — and inspired thousands of new investors to chase the next Flipkart.

Case Study 2: Byju's Boom and Bust

On the flip side, consider Byju's. Once valued at $22 billion, its unlisted shares were hot property. Brokers touted it as "India's next global education giant."

But in 2023–24, the company's valuation collapsed. Lawsuits, regulatory troubles, and poor financials turned investor dreams into nightmares. Those who bought unlisted shares at inflated prices saw their investments evaporate.

Byju's shows us that allure and reality can be very different.

The Cocktail Party Effect

At a social gathering, nothing makes an investor prouder than saying, "I own shares in XYZ — it's going to IPO next year." This subtle status boost adds to the allure.

It's not just about money. It's about identity. People love to feel smarter, earlier, and more insightful than the rest. Unlisted shares become a badge of that identity.

Why the Allure Matters

You might wonder: why spend a whole chapter on psychology and allure? Because if you don't understand the **emotional hooks**, you'll fall for them.

The unlisted market thrives on hype, FOMO, and stories. Rational analysis often takes a backseat. Beginners, especially, are pulled in by emotion first, numbers later.

By acknowledging the allure, you can step back and ask:

Am I investing because the fundamentals are strong, or because the story excites me?

Beginner's Reflection Exercise

Before you chase your first unlisted opportunity, sit down with a notebook and ask yourself honestly:

1. Do I want this stock because I believe in the business, or because I want to say I was "early"?
2. Am I being swayed by success stories without studying the failures?
3. If this company takes 10 years to succeed, am I willing to wait?
4. If this company fails, can I accept the loss without regret?

Your answers will reveal whether you're driven by reason or allure. Both matter, but reason should always have the final word.

Closing Thoughts

The private market is like a bright flame. It attracts investors with promises of 100x gains, insider status, and IPO riches. But as with any flame, if you get too close without protection, you'll get burned.

The allure is real, powerful, and unavoidable. But the wise investor learns to see through the dream — to separate the story from the substance.

In the next chapter, we'll confront the other side of the coin: **The Risks and Realities.** Because before you chase rewards, you must understand what you're truly up against.

Chapter - 4
The Risks and Realities

The Two Faces of the Market

Every coin has two sides. In Chapter 3, we explored the shining face of the private market — the allure of riches, exclusivity, and dream-chasing. Now, we must turn the coin over and confront the darker side: the risks and realities.

In fact, let's be blunt:

Most unlisted investments fail to deliver spectacular returns.

Some fail completely, wiping out your money.

And yet, most beginners ignore this truth because they are intoxicated by the dream. This chapter exists to sober you up — not to scare you away, but to help you step in with clear eyes.

Risk #1: Illiquidity – The Waiting Game

The number one difference between listed and unlisted stocks is **liquidity**.

- **Listed shares:** You buy today, you can sell tomorrow.
- **Unlisted shares:** You buy today… and may have to wait **5–10 years** before you can sell.

There's no open market. No daily buyers and sellers. Sometimes, even if you're willing to sell at a discount, there may be *no buyer at all*.

Story: A young IT professional bought shares of a fintech startup in 2017 for ₹3 lakhs, believing it would IPO soon. By 2023, the company was still private, struggling, and no one wanted to buy its shares. His money was frozen for years, and he eventually had to write off the investment.

💡 **Reality Check:** Before you invest, ask yourself:

"Am I willing to forget this money for at least 7–10 years?"

If the answer is no, don't invest in unlisted shares.

Risk #2: Lack of Transparency

Listed companies are required by law to disclose:

- Quarterly results
- Annual reports
- Auditor reviews
- Key management decisions

Unlisted companies? Not so much. Some may share financial statements with potential investors, but these are often unaudited or incomplete. Others may share nothing at all, leaving you to rely on rumours or "inside tips."

Example: In 2016, many investors bought unlisted shares of a real estate company on the promise of a coming IPO. The company delayed filings, hid losses, and quietly went bankrupt. Investors discovered the truth too late.

💡 **Reality Check:** If you can't verify numbers from at least 2 independent sources, treat the opportunity as suspicious.

Risk #3: Valuation Bubbles

In unlisted markets, **price is a matter of negotiation.** Unlike listed stocks, there's no live ticker showing supply and demand. Brokers may quote one price, employees another.

This leads to inflated valuations, especially in hot startups. A company valued at ₹10,000 crore in its last funding round might have little revenue to show for it.

Case Study: Byju's – Investors bought unlisted shares at sky-high valuations during its boom years. By 2023, the company's value had collapsed by more than 90%. Those investors now sit on near-worthless paper.

💡 **Reality Check:** Just because a big venture capital firm invested at a certain price doesn't mean you should. They may have negotiated different terms, protections, and exit rights that you don't get.

Risk #4: Scams and Frauds

Wherever there is money and information asymmetry, fraud follows. The unlisted market is no exception.

Scams can take many forms:

- **Fake shares:** Fraudsters selling forged share certificates.
- **Overpromising brokers:** Assuring IPO timelines that never materialise.
- **Ponzi-style deals:** Using new investors' money to pay old ones.

True Story (India, 2015): A group of investors bought "pre-IPO" shares of a reputed company through a shady broker. Later, they discovered the shares didn't exist — forged documents had been used. Their money vanished.

💡 **Reality Check:** Always verify the seller's legitimacy. Work only with SEBI-registered intermediaries or platforms.

Risk #5: Psychological Traps

The greatest risk is not the market, but your own mind.

- **FOMO (Fear of Missing Out):** "If I don't buy now, I'll miss the next Infosys."
- **Overconfidence:** "I spotted this company before anyone else, so I must be right."
- **Anchoring:** Believing a price is fair just because someone told you it was.

These traps cloud judgment. They turn smart professionals into reckless gamblers.

💡 **Reality Check:** Before buying, pause. Ask:

"If this were a listed company, would I still buy at this price based on fundamentals?"

Risk #6: Regulatory Blind Spots

In listed markets, regulators like SEBI (India) or SEC (US) keep a close eye. Insider trading, false reporting, and manipulation can still happen — but they are monitored.

Unlisted markets, however, operate in a grey zone. Many deals happen off-record, through networks or brokers. If things go wrong, legal recourse is slow, expensive, and often ineffective.

💡 **Reality Check:** Only invest amounts you can afford to lose without relying on regulators to rescue you.

Case Study: Theranos – The Global Lesson

Theranos, a U.S. healthcare startup, raised billions from private investors on the promise of revolutionary blood-testing technology. Its founder, Elizabeth Holmes, was celebrated as the next Steve Jobs.

But the technology didn't work. Financials were hidden. Audits were avoided. For years, investors believed the story. By the time the truth came out, Theranos was worthless, and investors lost everything.

Lesson: Even billionaires and experienced investors get fooled in unlisted markets. What chance does a beginner have without preparation?

The Illusion of "Safe" Big Names

Many beginners think: *If the company is big, it must be safe.* Not true. Large unlisted companies can also disappoint. Paytm's much-hyped IPO led to massive losses for those who bought shares at inflated pre-IPO prices.

Big name ≠ guaranteed returns.

The Harsh Truth in Numbers

According to global venture data:

- Roughly **70–80% of startups fail** within 5 years.
- About **10–15% provide moderate returns.**
- Only **1–5% deliver extraordinary wealth.**

This means: for every 100 unlisted bets, maybe 5 will make you rich — the rest will tie up or lose your money.

Beginner's Risk Filter

Before committing money, run the opportunity through this quick filter:

1. **Liquidity Test** – Can I hold for 7–10 years without selling?
2. **Verification Test** – Have I seen at least two independent documents confirming the company's health?
3. **Price Test** – Is this valuation reasonable compared to peers?

4. **Scam Test** – Do I know and trust the seller?
5. **Mindset Test** – Am I okay with losing 100% of this money if things go wrong?

If you answer "no" to any of these, pause. Better to miss an opportunity than to walk into a trap.

Closing Thoughts

The unlisted market is a high-risk, high-reward jungle. The dream is powerful, but the dangers are real. You must walk in like a climber entering Everest: eyes wide open, tools ready, fully aware that one misstep can be fatal.

In the next chapter, we'll shift from risks to **building the right mindset** — the psychological armour every investor needs before stepping deeper into this world.

Part - II

Investor Mindset

Chapter - 5
Investor Psychology

Why Psychology Matters More Than Math

When it comes to unlisted stocks, most beginners assume success is all about finding the "right" company. While that matters, the truth is: **your biggest enemy is not the company you invest in — it's yourself.**

History is full of investors who knew the numbers, understood the business, and still lost money because their emotions hijacked their decisions. In the private market, where uncertainty is higher and information is scarcer, psychology isn't just important — it's the difference between survival and ruin.

The Two Forces: Fear and Greed

The entire financial world runs on two engines: **fear** and **greed.**

- **Greed** whispers: What if this becomes the next Infosys? You'll be rich. Don't miss out.
- **Fear** whispers: What if it fails? You'll lose everything. Better stay away.

Successful investors don't eliminate these forces — they learn to manage them. Too much greed, and you chase every hot deal. Too much fear, and you never invest at all. Balance is the goal.

Patience: The Rare Superpower

The hardest part of unlisted investing is waiting. You can't refresh your trading app and see daily price moves. Months may pass without news. Years may pass without an IPO.

For most people, this waiting feels unbearable. They panic, sell too early, or lose hope. But patience is where the magic lies.

Story: One of Infosys's earliest employees was offered a chance to sell his shares for a small sum before the IPO. He refused, choosing patience. Years later, those same shares made him a millionaire.

💡 **Lesson:** In the unlisted world, impatience is your biggest cost.

The Danger of Overconfidence

Beginners often fall into the trap of believing they've spotted something others missed. "If I heard about this startup before my friends, I must be smarter."

But in reality, professional investors have often already looked at the same deal and passed for reasons you may not know. Overconfidence blinds you to risks.

💡 **Exercise:** Before investing, write down 3 reasons someone *smarter than you* might avoid this opportunity. This forces humility into your process.

Herd Mentality and FOMO

Have you noticed how restaurants feel more attractive when they're crowded? The same happens with investing. If everyone in your WhatsApp group or office is talking about a hot startup, you feel the urge to join.

This is **FOMO — the Fear of Missing Out.** It drives investors to overpay, skip due diligence, and chase hype.

Example: In the run-up to Paytm's IPO, investors scrambled to buy unlisted shares at sky-high prices. When the IPO flopped, many lost money.

💡 **Reality Check:** By the time an opportunity reaches the masses, the best gains are often already gone.

Loss Aversion: Why Losses Hurt More

Behavioural economists have shown that **losing ₹1,000 feels twice as painful as gaining ₹1,000 feels good.** This is called *loss aversion.*

In unlisted investing, this can paralyse you. After one bad experience, many beginners swear off the entire market forever. Others, desperate to "recover losses," throw more money at risky bets. Both reactions are emotional, not rational.

💡 **Rule of Thumb:** Treat every unlisted investment as tuition fees. Some lessons will cost money. The key is to pay small tuition (invest small) until you've truly learned.

Confirmation Bias: Hearing Only What You Want

When you like a company, you unconsciously look for news and opinions that confirm your belief — and ignore anything negative. This is called **confirmation bias.**

Example: An investor excited about Byju's in 2021 only read articles praising its global expansion. He ignored warnings about accounting irregularities. Today, his unlisted shares are worth a fraction of what he paid.

💡 **Exercise:** Before investing, deliberately search for criticism of the company. If you can't find any, you haven't looked hard enough.

Building an Investor's Mindset

So, what kind of mindset survives in the unlisted world? Here are the key traits:

1. **Curiosity** – A desire to dig deeper, ask questions, and learn continuously.
2. **Scepticism** – Not cynicism, but a healthy doubt about big claims.
3. **Patience** – The ability to wait for years without losing faith.
4. **Discipline** – Sticking to your budget and rules, even when tempted.
5. **Resilience** – Accepting losses as part of the journey, without giving up.

Sidebar: The Poker Analogy

Think of unlisted investing like poker. Both involve incomplete information, probability, and psychology. Good poker players don't win every hand — they win by playing smart, folding often, and staying calm under pressure. The same applies here.

A Simple Mental Framework

Before every investment, pause and ask yourself:

- **If this goes well, will it change my life?**
- **If this goes badly, will it ruin my life?**
- **Am I okay with either outcome?**

If the answer to the second question is "yes" (it could ruin your life), then you're investing too much. Scale down.

Beginner's Exercise: Investor Journal

Start a small notebook — your **Investor Journal.** Each time you consider an unlisted opportunity, write down:

- Why you're interested
- What excites you
- What scares you
- What could go wrong

Review it later. You'll be surprised how often your emotions, not the fundamentals, were driving your decision. Over time, this journal becomes your mirror and mentor.

Closing Thoughts

Numbers matter. Valuations matter. Legal contracts matter. But without the right psychology, none of it will save you. Fear, greed, and impatience will drag you into mistakes faster than any market risk.

If you learn to control yourself, you've already won half the battle.

In the next chapter, we'll deepen this discussion by exploring **Risk vs Reward** — how to measure potential outcomes realistically, so you don't get carried away by dreams or crippled by fears.

Chapter - 6
Risk Vs Reward

The Investor's Balancing Act

Every investment decision is a seesaw between two forces: **risk** and **reward.**

- **Reward** is the dream — the 10x or 100x gain that excites us.
- **Risk** is the nightmare — the chance of losing it all.

The challenge is not eliminating risk (that's impossible) but learning to **take smart risks** for worthwhile rewards. In the unlisted market, this balance is even more critical because the extremes are sharper: massive potential gains, but also the very real possibility of total loss.

Understanding Risk: What Can Go Wrong?

When you invest in an unlisted company, here's what you're really risking:

1. **Capital Loss** – The company fails, and your shares become worthless.
2. **Illiquidity** – You can't find a buyer for years, even if the company survives.
3. **Dilution** – The company raises more funds, and your ownership shrinks.

4. **Valuation Drops** – Even if the company grows, your entry price may have been too high.
5. **Fraud or Mismanagement** – Poor governance wipes out value.

In short:

"Your money is not only at risk of not growing—it's at risk of disappearing."

Understanding Reward: What Can Go Right?

On the flip side, the rewards are seductive:

1. **Massive Multipliers** – A small stake can grow 50x or 100x over a decade.
2. **Prestige of Early Entry** – Being an early backer of a famous company feels priceless.
3. **Life-Changing Exits** – IPOs, acquisitions, or buybacks can turn lakhs into crores.
4. **Portfolio Diversification** – Exposure to businesses outside the public markets.

But here's the catch: rewards are not guaranteed. They are *possible* outcomes, not *probable* ones.

Possibility vs Probability

This is the biggest mental mistake beginners make: **confusing possibility with probability.**

- It is *possible* that your ₹1 lakh investment in a startup turns into ₹1 crore.
- But it is far more *probable* that the company will fail, or deliver modest returns at best.

Professional investors think in probabilities, not fantasies. They know that if they invest in 10 startups, 7 will fail, 2 will do okay, and maybe 1 will explode. Their success comes from this portfolio approach — not from believing every deal is "the next big thing."

Case Study: The Angel Investor's Math

Ravi, an angel investor, put ₹10 lakhs into 10 different unlisted startups:

- 6 failed → 0 returns.
- 2 returned his money with small gains.
- 1 gave him 3x return.
- 1 became a unicorn → 50x return.

At first glance, his "hit rate" was poor (only 1 out of 10 was a blockbuster). But that single 50x return more than covered his losses and made him wealthy.

💡 **Lesson:** Success in unlisted investing comes from playing the odds, not chasing perfection.

The Asymmetry of Risk and Reward

In public markets, you may risk losing 20–30% in a bad stock. In unlisted markets, you risk losing **100%**.

But the reward side is also asymmetrical: in public markets, a "good" return might be 2–5x over years. In unlisted markets, it could be 20–100x.

This asymmetry is what makes the game worth playing—but only if you respect the downside.

How to Balance the Seesaw

Here are practical ways to balance risk and reward:

1. Small Ticket Sizes

Never put all your savings into one unlisted bet. Start small — think of it as "experimental money."

2. Portfolio Spread

Spread across different sectors and stages. Don't load up only on fintech or only on late-stage pre-IPO plays.

3. Exit Planning

Before you buy, ask: *How and when can I exit?* If there's no clear answer, think twice.

4. Valuation Discipline

Don't overpay. Enter at reasonable valuations — it increases your odds of positive returns.

The Casino vs the Investor

In a casino, the odds are stacked against you. In unlisted investing, the odds are tough but not hopeless. You can tilt them in your favour with knowledge, patience, and strategy.

But walk in blind, and you might as well be rolling dice.

Beginner's Framework: Risk-Reward Matrix

Before investing, draw a simple 2x2 box:

Risk	Reward	Example
High Risk + High Reward	Startup equity	Flipkart, Infosys (early days)
High Risk + Low Reward	Overhyped, overpriced shares	Many failed startups
Low Risk + High Reward	Rare, usually insider access	Early ESOPs of solid companies
Low Risk + Low Reward	Established unlisted firms with modest growth	Niche private companies

Your goal: avoid the "High Risk + Low Reward" box at all costs. That's where most beginners unknowingly invest.

Reflection Exercise

Before your next unlisted investment, write down:

- What is the worst-case scenario?
- What is the most likely scenario?
- What is the best-case scenario?
- Can I live with the worst, survive the likely, and wait for the best?

If the answer is yes, you're ready. If not, step back.

Closing Thoughts

Risk and reward are not enemies — they are dance partners. One pulls you forward, the other holds you back. The art of investing is learning when to let one lead and when to restrain the other.

In the unlisted world, the rewards are dazzling, but the risks are brutal. The investors who survive — and thrive—are those who think in probabilities, spread their bets, and always keep one foot grounded in reality.

In the next chapter, we'll explore **The Power of Long-Term Thinking** — why the biggest rewards in unlisted markets often belong to those willing to wait the longest.

Chapter - 7
The Power of Long-Term Thinking

The Forgotten Ingredient

Most beginners focus on "which stock to buy" and "at what price." Few think about **how long to hold.** Yet in unlisted investing, this single factor often determines the difference between disappointment and life-changing wealth.

The truth is simple: **the private market rewards the patient and punishes the restless.**

Why Time Matters More Here

In listed markets, you can buy and sell daily. Even short-term traders can make money. But in the unlisted world, short-term thinking is almost guaranteed to fail because:

- IPO timelines are unpredictable.
- Company growth takes years, not months.
- Liquidity is scarce — selling early usually means selling cheap.

If you expect quick profits, you're setting yourself up for frustration.

The Magic of Compounding

Compounding is often called the "eighth wonder of the world." In unlisted investing, compounding works not just on numbers, but on **business maturity.**

- A startup in year 1 may have ₹1 crore revenue.
- By year 5, it could be ₹50 crore.
- By year 10, ₹500 crore.

Your returns don't come linearly. They arrive in leaps — after years of slow, invisible progress.

💡 **Example:** An investor in Infosys in the 1990s didn't see dramatic gains in the first few years. But those who held on for decades saw wealth beyond imagination.

The Temptation to Exit Early

Patience sounds easy in theory, but in practice, it's brutally hard. You may face:

- Friends pressuring you to "book profits."
- Brokers offering to buy your shares at a modest premium.
- Media hype about competitors makes you doubt your choice.

Story: An employee at a tech startup sold his ESOPs early to fund a house purchase. He made a decent profit. Years later, when the company IPO'd, his colleagues who held on became millionaires. He often says, "I gained security, but lost fortune."

The lesson: short-term needs and impatience often rob you of long-term wealth.

The Psychology of Waiting

Why is waiting so hard? Because as humans, we are wired for **immediacy.** We prefer small rewards today over larger rewards tomorrow. Behavioural scientists call this *present bias.*

In unlisted investing, present bias makes you sell early, just to “lock in” a gain. But this often means you leave the biggest rewards on the table.

💡 **Exercise:** Before selling early, ask yourself: *Am I selling because the fundamentals changed, or because I’m simply tired of waiting?*

Case Study 1: The Infosys Millionaires

Many Infosys employees in the 1990s became wealthy not because they were financial geniuses, but because they **held on.** They endured years of waiting, resisted the urge to sell early, and let compounding do its work.

Patience turned ordinary middle-class professionals into extraordinary success stories.

Case Study 2: The Flipkart Exit

When Walmart acquired Flipkart, many early investors had already sold their stakes in secondary deals for modest returns. They made money, yes, but those who waited till the acquisition multiplied their wealth far more.

The early sellers often regret not trusting time.

The Bamboo Tree Lesson

The Chinese bamboo tree takes five years to break through the ground. For five years, you water it, nurture it, and see nothing. Then, in the sixth year, it grows **90 feet in six weeks.**

Unlisted companies are like bamboo. Years of invisible struggle may suddenly give way to explosive growth. If you quit watering too early, you'll never see the miracle.

Building the Patience Muscle

Patience is not natural — it must be trained. Here's how:

1. **Allocate "Dead Money"**

Only invest amounts you're willing to forget for years. Treat it like planting trees, not crops.

2. **Track Progress, Not Prices**

Since there's no daily ticker, focus on company updates—revenues, customers, milestones. That's where value builds.

3. **Journal Your Timeline**

Write down at the time of investment: *I'm willing to hold this for at least 7 years.* Revisit it whenever you feel restless.

4. **Diversify Patience**

If one company drags, others in your portfolio may move faster. A diversified basket helps you wait.

The Long-Term Investor's Edge

Here's the paradox:

- Most people *say* they're long-term investors.
- Very few actually are.

Because true long-term investing means:

- Enduring years of silence and doubt.
- Resisting the urge to sell early.
- Trusting the process when others give up.

If you can truly think in decades, not months, you gain an edge over 95% of investors who can't.

Beginner's Reflection Exercise

Answer honestly in your journal:

- Am I okay waiting 7–10 years for this company to deliver results?
- What life goals might tempt me to sell early (buying a house, emergency, etc.)?
- How can I plan my finances so I don't have to touch this money before its time?

The more you prepare for patience, the more likely you are to benefit from it.

Closing Thoughts

The unlisted market is not for sprinters. It's for marathoners. It rewards those who can see beyond the noise of the moment and hold their conviction through the fog of uncertainty.

Time is not your enemy here — it is your greatest ally. But only if you respect it.

In the next part of the book, we'll leave the mindset arena and step into the **mechanics of unlisted investing**—beginning with where to actually find these opportunities.

Part - III

The Mechanics of Unlisted Investing

Chapter - 8
Where to Find Unlisted Stocks

From Curiosity to Action

By now, you understand what unlisted stocks are, why they attract investors, and the psychological tools you need to survive. But a natural question arises: *Where do I actually find these opportunities?*

Unlike listed stocks, you can't just log into a trading app and buy. The unlisted world is fragmented, opaque, and often confusing. Finding the right entry point is half the battle.

The Main Sources of Unlisted Stocks

1. Employee Stock Ownership Plan (ESOP) Sales

Many startups reward employees with shares. Over time, employees may want to liquidate part of their holdings (to buy a house, pay debts, or diversify). These sales often become available to outside investors.

- **How it works:** Employees approach brokers or specialised platforms to sell their ESOPs.
- **Pros:** Often the only way to access early-stage winners.
- **Cons:** Limited supply, higher price volatility, and complex paperwork.

💡 **Example:** Early Paytm employees who sold part of their ESOPs in secondary sales before IPO created opportunities for retail investors.

2. Specialised Brokers and Dealers

There are firms whose entire business is connecting buyers and sellers of unlisted shares. They maintain networks of employees, early investors, and institutions looking to exit.

- **Pros:** Wider access to multiple companies, professional handling of paperwork.
- **Cons:** Risk of inflated pricing, hidden fees, or unreliable intermediaries. Always verify the broker's credentials (SEBI registration, reputation, reviews).

💡 **Tip:** Work with brokers who have a proven track record and don't hesitate to provide verifiable transaction documents.

3. Online Marketplaces & Platforms

In recent years, digital platforms have emerged to make unlisted investing more transparent. These platforms list available unlisted shares, often with indicative pricing, minimum investment size, and documentation support.

- **Examples (India):** UnlistedZone, Sharescart, EquityZen (US), Forge Global.
- **Pros:** Transparency, easier access for small investors, lower entry barriers.
- **Cons:** Prices may still vary widely from the "real" value; due diligence is still your responsibility.

💡 **Reality Check:** Just because a platform looks professional doesn't mean every deal is safe. The platform is a marketplace, not a guarantee.

4. Pre-IPO Placements

When a company prepares to go public, it often allows certain investors to buy shares in a **pre-IPO placement**. These shares may come with lock-in periods, but can be a gateway to high-quality companies.

- **Pros:** Access to mature businesses with clearer IPO timelines.
- **Cons:** Pricing may already be high due to IPO hype; lock-in rules may trap you if the IPO underperforms.

💡 **Example:** Investors who bought pre-IPO shares of IRCTC before its listing enjoyed strong listing gains. On the other hand, Paytm pre-IPO buyers suffered from heavy post-listing losses.

5. Private Deals and Investor Networks

Sometimes, opportunities circulate within private investor groups — angel networks, startup forums, LinkedIn connections, or even personal referrals.

- **Pros:** May provide access to very early-stage or exclusive opportunities.
- **Cons:** Highest risk of scams or misrepresentation. Requires strong verification.

💡 **Caution:** Never transfer money in private deals without clear documentation and legal agreements.

6. Venture Funds and Syndicates

If you're not comfortable picking individual stocks, you can join syndicates or angel funds that pool money from multiple investors to buy stakes in startups.

- **Pros:** Professional management, diversification, access to vetted deals.
- **Cons:** Higher minimum investment, management fees, and less control over which companies you back.

How Opportunities Reach You

Most unlisted opportunities come through **networks, not advertisements.** You'll often hear about deals via:

- A broker's call or email.
- An investor community sharing updates.
- An employee contact looking to liquidate.

This network-driven nature makes it exciting — but also dangerous. Without verification, you can easily fall for misinformation.

Sidebar: Beware of the "Too Easy" Deal

If someone approaches you saying, *"Guaranteed IPO, limited shares, act fast!"* — treat it as a red flag. Good opportunities rarely come with urgency. Scams often do.

The Grey Market Misunderstanding

Some beginners confuse **grey market trading** (where IPO shares are bought and sold before listing) with unlisted investing. They are not the same:

- Grey market = short-term speculation on IPO listing gains.
- Unlisted shares = long-term ownership in a private company.

Don't mistake one for the other.

Evaluating the Source: A Quick Checklist

Before you commit, ask yourself:

1. **Who is selling to me?** (Employee, broker, platform?)
2. **Are they regulated or registered?** (SEBI/SEC checks?)
3. **Is there verifiable documentation?** (Demat transfers, legal contracts?)
4. **How is the price determined?** (Last funding round? Negotiated?)
5. **What's my exit path?** (IPO, buyback, secondary market?)

If you can't answer these clearly, step back.

Case Study: The Broker Trap

In 2018, a group of investors in Mumbai bought "pre-IPO" shares of a reputed firm from an unverified broker. They were promised guaranteed listing gains. When the IPO didn't happen, the broker disappeared. The investors were left with worthless paper and no legal recourse.

💡 **Lesson:** The source of your shares is just as important as the shares themselves.

Beginner's Exercise: Mapping Your Access Points

Take a notebook and list:

- Brokers/platforms you know.
- Investor networks or communities you belong to.
- Employees or founders you know personally.

This will show you your **entry map**. Over time, strengthen these access points — but always verify them before use.

Closing Thoughts

Finding unlisted stocks is not as simple as opening a trading app. It's a world of relationships, brokers, and niche platforms. Access is both the opportunity and the challenge.

But remember: just because you *can* access an opportunity doesn't mean you *should.* The next chapters will teach you how to judge what's worth buying, what's overpriced, and what's a trap.

Next up: **Understanding Valuations** — where we dive into the tricky art of figuring out what an unlisted company is actually worth.

Chapter - 9
Understanding Valuations

Why Valuation Matters More Than the Story

In unlisted investing, the story is seductive: visionary founders, disruptive products, the next big thing. But stories don't pay bills. **Valuation determines whether you make money or lose it.**

Buying a great company at the wrong price can be just as damaging as buying a bad company. The private market is notorious for inflated valuations, so learning how to value is your shield.

The Basics: What Is Valuation?

Valuation is simply an estimate of what a company is worth today. Think of it like buying a house:

- Two similar houses in the same area may have wildly different asking prices.
- If you overpay, it may take decades before you break even.
- If you buy at the right price, you can profit even in a modest market.

Unlisted stocks are no different.

Common Valuation Methods (Simplified for Beginners)

1. Comparable Company Analysis (Comps)

Look at similar companies (public or private) and see what multiples they trade at.

- Example: If listed fintech companies are valued at **5x revenue**, and your target startup has ₹100 crore revenue, a fair value may be ₹500 crore.

Pros: Simple, widely used.

Cons: Assumes peers are fairly valued (not always true).

2. Price-to-Earnings (P/E) Ratio

Divide the share price by earnings per share (EPS).

- **Example:** A company earning ₹10 crore annually with 1 crore shares outstanding = EPS ₹10. If the share trades at ₹200, P/E = 20.

Compare with industry P/Es. If peers are at 15, maybe you're overpaying.

3. Price-to-Book (P/B) Ratio

Compares market price to book value (assets minus liabilities).

- Useful for banks, NBFCs, and asset-heavy firms.
- **Example:** If book value per share is ₹100, and shares trade at ₹300, P/B = 3.

4. Discounted Cash Flow (DCF)

Estimate future cash flows and discount them to today's value.

- **Example:** If you expect ₹10 crore annual profit growing 20% annually for 10 years, you bring those profits back to today's value using a discount rate (say 12%).

Pros: Theoretically sound.

Cons: Easily manipulated by unrealistic assumptions.

5. Last Funding Round Price

Startups often use their last VC funding round as the basis for valuation.

- **Example:** If a venture fund bought at ₹1,000/share, brokers may offer you the same price.

But remember: VCs often have **preferential rights** (liquidation preference, anti-dilution, etc.) that retail investors don't get. Paying the same price without protections may be unfair.

Valuation Red Flags to Watch Out For

1. **Sky-High Multiples** – If a company is valued at 50x revenue with no profits, beware.
2. **Hype Premium** – If a company is in a hot sector (like edtech during COVID), expect inflated prices.

3. **Flat Revenues, Rising Valuations** – If the business isn't growing but the price keeps rising, it's a bubble.

4. **Lack of Transparency** – If financials aren't shared, you're betting blind.

Case Study: Byju's Valuation Bubble

At its peak, Byju's was valued at $22 billion despite mounting losses. Investors bought unlisted shares at high premiums, believing "scale equals value." When reality hit — slowing growth, mounting debt, regulatory scrutiny — valuations collapsed by over 90%.

💡 **Lesson:** Revenue growth without profitability can sustain only for so long. Always ask: *What is the company actually earning?*

Case Study: IRCTC Pre-IPO

Before IRCTC was listed, pre-IPO shares were available at ₹300–400. Investors who understood its monopoly and cash-rich model knew this was undervalued. Upon listing, shares surged past ₹1,000.

💡 **Lesson:** Strong fundamentals + fair entry price = wealth creation.

The "Greater Fool" Trap

Some investors justify high prices by saying,

"I'll sell to someone else at an even higher price."

This works… until the music stops. When no "greater fool" arrives, you're the one left holding overpriced shares.

How Beginners Can Approach Valuation (Without Being Experts)

1. **Start with Revenue** – Is it growing? At what rate?
2. **Check Profitability** – Is there profit, or only losses disguised as "growth"?
3. **Compare Multiples** – Use listed peers as a benchmark.
4. **Look at Cash Flows** – Is the company burning cash, or generating it?
5. **Ask: Who Else Invested?** – Big-name investors help, but don't follow blindly.

Tools You Can Use

- **Annual Reports / MCA Filings (India)** – Basic financials available.
- **Startup Databases** – Tracxn, Crunchbase, etc.
- **Broker Reports** – Platforms often provide snapshots (but verify).
- **Your Own Spreadsheet** – Even a simple Excel with revenue, profits, and multiples can give clarity.

Beginner's Checklist: Am I Overpaying?

1. Is this price higher than what VCs paid in the last round?
2. Do I have fewer rights than those investors?

3. Does this valuation assume "perfection" in growth?
4. How does this compare with listed peers?
5. If the IPO happens at a lower valuation, will I still make money?

If your answers raise doubts, don't buy. In unlisted investing, **the price you pay determines the future you get.**

Closing Thoughts

Valuation is part art, part science. You don't need to be a CFA to succeed, but you must avoid being blind. Numbers don't tell the whole story, but they keep you grounded when the story is too sweet.

In the next chapter, we'll take the next step: **Due Diligence Made Simple** — how to check beyond numbers, look at business models, management credibility, and avoid traps.

Chapter - 10
Due Diligence Made Simple

Why due Diligence Matters

A glossy pitch deck, a famous founder, or glowing news articles may tempt you to invest. But as Warren Buffett once said:

"Never invest in a business you don't understand."

In unlisted investing, information is limited. Companies don't have to disclose quarterly earnings, and brokers rarely tell you the full story. This makes **Due Diligence (DD)** your most powerful weapon.

Think of DD as a background check before marriage. You wouldn't marry someone just because they look good in photos. You'd ask questions, meet their family, and check their history. Investing in unlisted companies deserves the same caution.

The Three Pillars of Due Diligence

1. Financial Due Diligence – Numbers Don't Lie (Unless They Do)

Look at the company's financial health:

- **Revenue growth:** Is it increasing year after year, or flat/declining?

- **Profitability:** Is the company making money, or burning cash?
- **Cash flow:** Paper profits don't matter if there's no real cash.
- **Debt levels:** High debt = high risk, especially for private firms.

💡 **Example:** A consumer startup showed impressive revenue, but deeper checks revealed it was spending ₹120 to earn ₹100. Growth looked exciting, but losses were unsustainable.

2. Business Due Diligence – The Engine of Growth

Ask: *How does this company actually make money?*

- **Business model:** Clear or confusing?
- **Customer base:** Growing, loyal, or one-time buyers?
- **Competition:** Does it have a moat (something hard to copy)?
- **Scalability:** Can it grow nationwide or globally, or is it stuck locally?

💡 **Case Study:** IRCTC had a monopoly in railway ticketing. Scalability was obvious, and the moat was unbeatable. That's why pre-IPO investors made strong returns.

3. Management Due Diligence – The Human Factor

A great business in the wrong hands is a disaster. Study the people behind it:

- **Background:** Do founders have credibility, or a history of failed ventures/frauds?
- **Skin in the game:** Are they personally invested, or just spending investor money?
- **Governance:** Do they respect minority investors, or sideline them?
- **Transparency:** Do they willingly share updates or avoid tough questions?

💡 **Red Flag Example:** In Byju's, concerns about governance and transparency were ignored during the boom years. Later, these became the very reasons valuations crashed.

The Simplified DD Framework (For Beginners)

Here's a quick 5-step method anyone can use:

1. **Collect Documents** – Ask for audited financials, ROC filings (in India), or investor presentations.
2. **Check Revenues & Losses** – Are they sustainable? Is the trend up or down?
3. **Google Deep Dive** – Search for news, employee reviews, lawsuits, and complaints.
4. **Cross-Verify** – Don't rely on one broker. Check 2–3 sources for the same story.

5. **Talk to Users/Employees** – If possible, get first-hand feedback on the product/service.

Red Flags to Watch Out For

- **Aggressive promises:** "Guaranteed IPO in 12 months."
- **Unrealistic growth:** "We'll grow 10x in one year."
- **High customer churn:** Many people try, few return.
- **Founder exits:** If founders are quietly selling, beware.
- **Opaque structures:** Complex holding companies with no clarity.

💡 **Case Study:** A health-tech startup raised funds on big promises. Quick DD revealed lawsuits from ex-employees and vendors. Many investors ignored the signs and later regretted it.

The Taxi Test

If you can't explain a company's business to a taxi driver in two minutes, you probably don't understand it well enough. Complexity often hides weakness.

Tools for Due Diligence (Beginner-Friendly)

- **India:**
  - ✓ MCA (Ministry of Corporate Affairs) filings for financials.
  - ✓ Platforms like Tofler, ZaubaCorp.

- **Global:**
    - ✓ Crunchbase, PitchBook, CB Insights.
- **Generic:**
    - ✓ LinkedIn (check employee reviews and attrition).
    - ✓ Glassdoor (culture and management).
    - ✓ News aggregators (Google Alerts on company/founders).

Case Study: Theranos – The Missed Due Diligence

Theranos fooled billionaires, but not everyone. Some medical experts raised early doubts: "If this tech worked, why won't they show peer-reviewed data?" That simple DD question could have saved investors billions.

💡 **Lesson:** If a company avoids transparency, it's often hiding a weakness.

Beginner's Exercise: Run a Mini-DD on a Known Brand

Pick a well-known unlisted company (e.g., Reliance Retail before IPO buzz).

- Look up its last available financials.
- Search for 5 news articles about it.
- Check Glassdoor for employee feedback.
- Ask: Would I still invest after seeing this?

This practice builds your DD muscle before risking real money.

The "Layering" Approach to DD

Think of due diligence like peeling an onion:

1. **Outer layer:** Public news, websites, press releases.
2. **Middle layer:** Financial statements, industry data, competitor analysis.
3. **Core:** Conversations with insiders, employees, or industry experts.

Most beginners stop at the outer layer. Serious investors dig deeper.

Closing Thoughts

Due diligence won't guarantee success — but skipping it almost guarantees failure. In the unlisted world, you don't have the safety net of daily disclosures and strict regulators. The responsibility is yours.

Remember: you're not just buying shares. You're buying into people, ideas, and a future. Check carefully before you write the cheque.

In the next chapter, we'll move into **The Legal Side** — the paperwork, rights, and regulations you must understand to protect yourself.

Chapter - 11
The Legal Side

Why Legal Awareness Matters

The private market thrives on stories and promises. But when disputes arise — about ownership, exit, or valuation — only one thing matters: **the contract.**

Too many retail investors enter deals with nothing but WhatsApp messages or verbal assurances. Later, when companies delay IPOs, brokers vanish, or disputes emerge, they realise they had no enforceable rights.

Legal literacy is not optional. It's your seatbelt in a high-speed car.

The Basic Legal Documents You Must Know

1. Shareholder Agreement (SHA)

This is the backbone of your investment. It defines:

- How many shares do you own?
- What rights you have (voting, dividends, information access).
- What happens in the case of mergers, buybacks, or liquidation?

💡 **Tip:** Always insist on reading the SHA, not just a broker's summary.

2. Share Purchase Agreement (SPA)

This is the contract between the buyer (you) and the seller (employee, broker, or another shareholder). It records the terms of sale:

- Number of shares.
- Price per share.
- Transfer conditions.
- Payment method.

Without an SPA, you risk paying money without a guaranteed transfer of shares.

3. Share Certificates / Demat Entry

Your ownership must be documented either as:

- A **physical share certificate** (rare today), or
- An entry in your **Demat account** (preferred).

If the transfer doesn't show up in Demat, you don't truly own the shares.

4. Lock-In Agreements

Pre-IPO shares often come with a lock-in period (SEBI rule in India, SEC rules in the US) where you cannot sell for 6–12 months post-IPO.

💡 **Example:** Many Paytm pre-IPO investors couldn't sell during the initial crash due to lock-ins. By the time lock-in expired, prices had already fallen sharply.

5. Rights of Different Investors

Not all shares are equal.

- **Venture Capitalists** often get "preferred shares" with rights like liquidation preference, anti-dilution, and board seats.
- **Retail investors** usually get "common shares" with fewer protections.

This means paying the same price as a VC does not mean you're on equal footing.

Regulatory Frameworks to Be Aware Of

In India (SEBI):

- **Unlisted trading is legal** but must comply with SEBI regulations.
- **Demat requirement**: Transfers should ideally be via NSDL/CDSL.
- **Pre-IPO lock-in**: Minimum 6 months.
- **Insider trading** rules apply even before IPO.

In the US (SEC):

- Only "accredited investors" (high income/net worth) are allowed in many private deals.
- Platforms like EquityZen and Forge Global provide legal compliance.

💡 **Lesson:** Always check if you are legally eligible to invest.

Common Legal Traps

1. Verbal Promises

"Don't worry, IPO is coming next year." If it's not in writing, it doesn't exist.

2. Fake or Forged Certificates

Fraudsters issue fake share certificates. Only Demat verification guarantees authenticity.

3. Side Agreements

Some brokers create "side letters" promising exits. These are unenforceable in court.

4. Lack of Disclosure

Companies may hide ongoing lawsuits or liabilities unless you ask.

Case Study: The ESOP Confusion

An employee of a fintech startup sold part of his ESOPs to a retail investor. Later, the company claimed the shares were under a "lock-in" and invalidated the transfer. The buyer lost his money.

💡 **Lesson:** Always confirm with the company whether ESOP shares are transferable before buying.

The "Signature Test"

Before you transfer money, ask: *Who has signed my document?*

- If it's not the actual shareholder or company official, beware.
- Brokers cannot transfer ownership unless they themselves are the legal owner.

Protecting Yourself: Best Practices

1. Work Through Demat

Always prefer electronic transfer over paper certificates.

2. Demand Documentation

SPA, SHA, Demat confirmation — don't settle for "assurances."

3. Check Company Consent

Some private firms require board approval for share transfers. Verify this.

4. Understand Lock-In

Know exactly how long you'll be unable to sell.

5. Hire a Legal Advisor (for bigger deals)

Spending a few thousand on a lawyer can save lakhs later.

Beginner's Legal Checklist

Before you say yes:

- Do I have a signed **Share Purchase Agreement**?
- Is my ownership recorded in the **Demat** or official registers?
- Have I checked for **lock-in restrictions**?
- Do I know if these are **common shares** or **preferred shares**?
- Is everything I've been promised **written in the contract**?

If any box remains unchecked, don't proceed.

Closing Thoughts

In the unlisted jungle, legal documents are your shield. Without them, you are defenceless against fraud, disputes, and broken promises.

Numbers may decide your potential profit, but **contracts decide whether you even own what you think you own.**

In the next chapter, we'll move from the legal side to strategy: **How to Start Small** — a beginner's step-by-step guide to making your very first unlisted investment safely.

Part - IV

Strategies & Playbooks

Chapter - 12
How to Start Small

The Beginner's Dilemma

By now, you've learned the opportunities, the risks, the psychology, the valuation basics, and the legal side. But here's the problem most beginners face:

"I understand the theory, but how do I actually start? And how much should I invest?"

This chapter is your **training ground.** Think of it as dipping your toes in the water before diving into the deep end.

Why Start Small?

- **Risk Control:** You're still learning. Mistakes will happen. Smaller amounts = smaller losses.
- **Experience First:** Theory is nothing until you see how deals actually work.
- **Emotional Training:** Handling uncertainty with ₹25,000 is easier than with ₹5 lakhs.
- **Building Confidence:** Small wins prepare you for bigger steps.

💡 **Rule of Thumb:** Treat your first 2–3 unlisted investments as **learning tuition**, not wealth generators.

Step 1: Decide Your Budget

- Invest only **disposable capital** — money you can afford to forget for 5–10 years.
- A good starting point: **5–10% of your total investment portfolio.**
- Within that, begin with a **single small ticket size.**

💡 **Example:** If you have ₹10 lakhs across savings, mutual funds, and stocks, allocate only ₹50,000–₹1 lakh for unlisted shares in the first year.

Step 2: Choose Your First Type of Investment

Not all unlisted shares are equal. For beginners, start where risk is manageable:

1. **Pre-IPO Shares of Established Firms**
   - Safer than startups, clearer IPO timeline.
   - Example: Buying pre-IPO shares of NSE, IRCTC, or Reliance Retail.
2. **ESOPs of Mature Startups**
   - Employees selling part of their vested stock in well-known firms.
   - Example: Shares of Paytm or Zomato before IPO.

❌ **Avoid very early-stage startups initially.** These are high-risk and need advanced DD skills.

Step 3: Pick the Right Channel

Choose a safe source for your first deal:

- A reputed **broker/platform** with SEBI registration.
- ESOP sale facilitated by a known employee + verified documentation.

❌ Avoid WhatsApp groups and random intermediaries for your first investment.

Step 4: Understand the Process (Mini Walkthrough)

Here's how a typical small unlisted investment works:

1. **You contact a broker/platform.**
2. They share available companies and indicative pricing.
3. You select, sign a **Share Purchase Agreement (SPA).**
4. You transfer money (through official bank transfer, not cash).
5. Shares get transferred to your **Demat account** (or physical certificate if older).
6. You verify ownership.

Once done, you're officially an unlisted shareholder.

Step 5: Set Realistic Expectations

Your first investment may not make you rich. Treat it as a **learning experience.** You're practising how to:

- Read agreements.
- Verify Demat transfers.

- Experience the illiquidity.
- Track company progress.

Even if returns are modest (say, 20–30% over the years), the real win is confidence and skill.

Case Study: Rohan's First ₹50,000

Rohan, a 28-year-old engineer in Pune, wanted to try unlisted investing. He allocated ₹50,000 into pre-IPO shares of NSE via a reputed platform.

- He carefully checked documents, waited for 8 months, and eventually sold during a liquidity window for ₹65,000.
- The 30% return was good, but more importantly, Rohan learned the process end-to-end.
- Now, he's prepared to scale gradually into larger bets.

💡 **Lesson:** Start small, learn big.

Sidebar: Avoid the "All-In" Temptation

Many beginners get excited and throw ₹2–3 lakhs into their very first deal. That's like learning to swim by jumping into the deep ocean. The market will punish impatience.

Small tickets are training wheels. Use them until you're stable.

A Simple Beginner's Playbook

1. **First Year** – 1–2 small investments in safe categories (₹25k–₹50k each).
2. **Second Year** – Expand to 3–4 investments, including 1 mid-risk startup.

3. **Third Year Onwards** – Build a small portfolio of 5–7 unlisted stocks across sectors.

This gradual approach gives you both exposure and resilience.

Beginner's Checklist: My First Deal

Before committing, tick these boxes:

- ✓ Investment is ≤10% of my portfolio.
- ✓ I understand the company's business in simple terms.
- ✓ I verified all documents and the Demat transfer.
- ✓ I am okay waiting 5–7 years.
- ✓ I'm treating this as tuition, not a jackpot.

If you check all 5, you're ready.

Closing Thoughts

Every expert investor was once a beginner. The difference is that they started small, survived mistakes, and gradually built wisdom.

Your first unlisted investment won't change your life — but it will change your confidence. It's the first brick in a much larger foundation.

In the next chapter, we'll explore how to avoid over-concentration by building a balanced portfolio: **Diversification in the Private Market.**

Chapter - 13
Diversification in the Private Market

Why Diversification Is Non-Negotiable

Unlisted investing is like farming. If you plant seeds in only one field and a storm wipes it out, you lose everything. But if you spread seeds across different fields, soil types, and crops, you improve your chances that at least some will thrive.

In private markets, **most companies fail.** The odds are brutal. Diversification isn't just a good idea — it's survival.

The Harsh Statistics

Globally, studies show that out of 10 startups:

- 6–7 fail completely.
- 2–3 return only modest gains.
- 1 becomes a big winner that covers all losses and more.

If you only invest in one or two, odds are you'll pick the failures. Diversification ensures you stay in the game long enough to catch a winner.

Different Dimensions of Diversification

1. By Company Stage

- **Early-Stage Startups:** High risk, high potential (10x–100x).
- **Growth-Stage Startups:** Some traction, more visibility (3x–10x).
- **Pre-IPO Companies:** Lower risk, clearer exits (1.5x–3x).

💡 Strategy: Mix across stages. For example, 60% in safer pre-IPO/growth firms, 40% in riskier early-stage.

2. By Sector

Don't load up only on fintech, edtech, or e-commerce just because they're trending. Spread across:

- Tech (fintech, SaaS, AI)
- Consumer goods
- Healthcare/Pharma
- Logistics/Infrastructure
- Niche monopolies (like IRCTC was pre-IPO)

💡 Case Study: During COVID-19, edtech boomed, but later crashed. Investors who also had healthcare and consumer startups balanced their portfolios.

3. By Ticket Size

Your investments don't all need to be equal. Use a **tiered approach:**

- Small tickets in high-risk startups.
- Medium tickets in growth companies.
- Larger tickets in safer pre-IPO opportunities.

This way, you maximise learning while controlling downside.

4. By Geography (Optional for advanced investors)

If possible, diversify across markets. A crisis in one country may not affect another. Platforms like EquityZen (US) or Seedrs (UK) provide access to international opportunities.

Sidebar: The "Egg Basket" Misquote

Everyone knows the saying: *"Don't put all your eggs in one basket."* But few know the second part, often ignored: *"...but if you must, watch that basket very closely."*

Diversification protects you from failure, but spreading too thin without monitoring also weakens results. Balance is the key.

Case Study: Radhika's Balanced Portfolio

Radhika, a 35-year-old corporate professional, allocated ₹5 lakhs into unlisted shares:

- ₹2 lakhs into pre-IPO shares of NSE and Reliance Retail.
- ₹1.5 lakhs into growth-stage consumer startups.
- ₹1 lakh into two early-stage tech startups.
- ₹50,000 into an angel fund syndicate.

5 years later:

- 2 early-stage startups failed.
- The consumer startups gave modest 2x returns.

- NSE IPO delivered strong gains.
- Reliance Retail valuation surged.

Her overall portfolio doubled — not because every bet won, but because **diversification absorbed failures and let winners shine.**

The Danger of Over-Diversification

While spreading is good, too much diversification is also a problem. If you put ₹10,000 in 50 companies, you won't be able to track or meaningfully benefit from winners.

💡 **Sweet Spot:** For most beginners, a portfolio of **5–10 unlisted companies** are enough.

Beginner's Framework: Building a Starter Portfolio

Suppose you have ₹2 lakhs for unlisted investing:

- **₹1 lakh (50%)** → Safer pre-IPO companies (e.g., NSE, LIC before listing).
- **₹60,000 (30%)** → Growth-stage startups with clear traction.
- **₹40,000 (20%)** → Early-stage high-risk bets.

This structure balances excitement with safety.

Reflection Exercise: My Diversification Map

Draw a simple pie chart of your planned portfolio:

- What % in early-stage vs growth vs pre-IPO?
- What % across sectors?
- What % is one company taking?

If one slice dominates, rebalance.

Closing Thoughts

In the private market, you don't control outcomes. But you do control your spread. Diversification ensures that one failure doesn't sink your entire ship. It allows you to survive long enough to catch the rare winners that make the journey worthwhile.

In the next chapter, we'll explore the other side of the coin: **Exit Strategies** — because investing is only half the game. Knowing how and when to exit is what converts paper wealth into real money.

Chapter - 14
Exit Strategies

Why Exits Matter More Than Entries

In unlisted investing, getting in is easy. Brokers and platforms will happily sell you shares. But getting out? That's the challenge.

Unlike listed stocks, you can't just click "sell." Exits in private markets require **planning, patience, and timing.** Without a strategy, you may be stuck holding valuable paper with no buyer.

The Main Exit Routes

1. Initial Public Offering (IPO)

The most celebrated exit path. When a company lists, your unlisted shares become tradable on the stock exchange.

- **Pros:** Liquidity, visibility, prestige.
- **Cons:** IPO delays, lock-in periods (6–12 months), post-listing price crashes.

💡 **Example:** IRCTC pre-IPO investors enjoyed massive listing gains.

✕ **Counter-Example:** Paytm pre-IPO buyers saw their shares drop 50%+ post-listing.

2. Buybacks by the Company

Some companies repurchase shares from employees or early investors at set valuations.

- **Pros:** Clean exit, backed by the company itself.
- **Cons:** Buybacks may be limited; and prices may not be attractive.

💡 **Example:** Infosys conducted periodic ESOP buybacks, creating steady liquidity for employees.

3. Acquisition / Merger Exit

When a larger company acquires the firm, shareholders often get paid in cash or swapped equity.

- **Pros:** Can deliver windfall exits (like Flipkart → Walmart).
- **Cons:** Rare and unpredictable. You can't "plan" for an acquisition.

4. Secondary Market Sales

You sell your shares to another private investor via a broker or platform.

- **Pros:** Flexibility, available even before IPO.
- **Cons:** Buyers may negotiate hard; prices may be much lower than you expect.

💡 **Case Study:** Many Zomato employees sold shares in the secondary market before IPO to diversify their wealth.

5. Private Equity / Venture Fund Exits

Sometimes, institutional investors buy stakes from smaller holders. This usually happens in larger rounds when the company raises fresh funding.

- **Pros:** Institutional buyers = more reliable.
- **Cons:** Rare for retail investors; usually negotiated at scale.

Timing Is Everything

Getting the exit route right is only half the game. The other half is **when** you exit.

- Exit **too early** → You miss exponential growth.
- Exit **too late** → You face valuation collapse or dilution.

💡 **Example:** Some early Flipkart investors sold small stakes for modest profits before the Walmart deal. Later, they regretted missing the 100x windfall.

💡 **Counter-Example:** Byju's investors who refused early exit offers at inflated prices are now stuck with losses.

Sidebar: Paper Wealth vs Real Wealth

Unlisted shares can look impressive on paper — "I own ₹50 lakhs worth of XYZ startup." But unless you exit, it's just numbers. Real wealth is only created at exit.

The Lock-In Trap

Many investors don't realise their shares may be locked post-IPO. In India, SEBI mandates:

- Pre-IPO investors → Minimum 6 months lock-in.
- Promoters → Longer lock-in (up to 3 years).

If the stock crashes during your lock-in, your paper gains may evaporate.

💡 **Lesson:** Always ask about lock-in terms before buying.

Building an Exit Plan (Beginner-Friendly)

1. **Before Buying:** Ask yourself — what's the most likely exit path (IPO, buyback, secondary)?
2. **Know the Timeline:** IPO planned in 2 years? Acquisition talks? No visibility?
3. **Set a Target:** At what valuation/price will you sell? Don't just "hold forever."
4. **Stay Flexible:** Market conditions may force changes. Be willing to exit early if risks rise.

Case Study: The NSE Pre-IPO Journey

Investors who bought NSE shares in the unlisted market years ago have waited patiently for the IPO, which has been delayed multiple times due to regulatory issues. Some sold in secondary markets for modest gains, while others continue holding, hoping for a bigger payday.

💡 **Lesson:** Exit plans must adapt to delays. Don't tie up all your liquidity in one uncertain timeline.

Beginner's Checklist: My Exit Strategy

Before you commit money, tick these boxes:

- Do I know my likely exit route (IPO, buyback, secondary)?
- Am I clear on lock-in rules?
- Have I set a target return where I'll sell?
- Do I have backup options if IPO delays?
- Will this exit give me **cash in hand**, not just paper profits?

Closing Thoughts

In unlisted investing, the art of exiting is as important as the science of entering. The difference between a dream and a disaster often comes down to your ability to plan, wait, and act wisely at the right moment.

Remember: the goal is not just to own exciting companies — it's to convert ownership into real wealth.

In the next chapter, we'll zoom out and study **Case Studies of Wins and Failures** — stories from both sides of the spectrum that carry priceless lessons for every investor.

Chapter - 15

Case Studies of Winners and Failures

Why Stories Matter

Theories and checklists are useful, but nothing teaches like real-world stories. Every great investor carries scars from failures and pride from wins. By studying them, you get to "borrow" their experience without paying the same tuition fee.

Let's walk through a few landmark case studies — some inspiring, some cautionary — that illustrate the reality of unlisted investing.

Win #1: Flipkart – The Unicorn Fairy Tale

- **The Story:** Founded in 2007 as a small online bookstore in Bengaluru, Flipkart grew into India's biggest e-commerce giant.
- **The Opportunity:** Early investors, including Tiger Global and Accel Partners, entered when valuations were modest. Employees with ESOPs also got stakes early.
- **The Exit:** In 2018, Walmart acquired Flipkart for $16 billion. Early backers multiplied their money many times over. Some employees became crorepatis overnight.

💡 **Lesson:** Early-stage investments can deliver life-changing wealth if the company becomes a market leader. But such fairy tales are rare — for every Flipkart, dozens of startups die quietly.

Win #2: IRCTC – The Monopoly Advantage

- **The Story:** The Indian Railway Catering and Tourism Corporation was a government-owned monopoly with clear revenue streams.
- **The Opportunity:** Pre-IPO investors could buy shares around ₹300–400.
- **The Exit:** On listing in 2019, IRCTC soared to over ₹1,000 within days, creating enormous listing gains.

💡 **Lesson:** Not every win comes from risky startups. Mature, monopoly-driven pre-IPO firms can deliver safe, strong returns.

Failure #1: Byju's – The Valuation Mirage

- **The Story:** Once the world's most valuable edtech company, Byju's raised billions and expanded aggressively.
- **The Opportunity:** At its peak, unlisted shares were sold at valuations above $20 billion. Retail investors rushed in, believing the hype.
- **The Collapse:** By 2023–24, accounting issues, mounting losses, and governance troubles caused valuation to drop by over 90%. Investors who entered at inflated prices saw their wealth vanish.

💡 **Lesson:** Valuation discipline is everything. A good story cannot save you if you enter at the wrong price.

Failure #2: Theranos – The Global Fraud

- **The Story:** A US healthcare startup claimed it could run hundreds of tests from a single drop of blood. Founder Elizabeth Holmes became a Silicon Valley star.
- **The Opportunity:** High-profile investors, including billionaires, backed it. Retail investors never got direct access, but the lesson remains universal.
- **The Collapse:** The technology didn't work. After whistleblowers exposed the fraud, Theranos collapsed, wiping out billions. Holmes was convicted of fraud.

💡 **Lesson:** Even smart investors can be fooled by hype and secrecy. If a company avoids transparency, run.

Mixed Case: Paytm – The IPO Rollercoaster

- **The Story:** Paytm revolutionised digital payments in India and became a household name.
- **The Opportunity:** Pre-IPO investors bought shares at high valuations amid massive buzz.
- **The Exit:** On listing in 2021, the IPO priced at ₹2,150. Within months, shares crashed 60%. Many pre-IPO investors were stuck in lock-ins and booked losses.

- **The Long View:** The business still has value, but early buyers who expected quick IPO gains were punished.

💡 **Lesson:** Big brands don't guarantee smooth exits. Timing and valuation matter as much as the company's story.

Survivorship Bias

When you hear about wins like Flipkart or Infosys, remember you're hearing only about the survivors. For every success story, 50 failures never make headlines. Don't let survivorship bias trick you into thinking wins are common.

The Common Patterns Behind Wins

- Market leaders with strong growth.
- Reasonable entry valuations.
- Clear business models.
- Patience from investors.

The Common Patterns Behind Failures

- Overhyped valuations.
- Weak fundamentals hidden by storytelling.
- Poor governance or transparency.
- Impatience (rushing for exits).

Beginner's Reflection Exercise

Think of three companies you admire today (listed or unlisted). For each, ask:

- What if I had invested early?
- What could have gone wrong?
- Which lessons from the case studies apply?

This simple thought experiment keeps you grounded when evaluating new deals.

Closing Thoughts

Wins and failures are two sides of the same coin. The private market is full of both, and you will experience both if you invest long enough. The key is to learn from others' scars so your own losses are smaller and your wins larger.

In the next part of the book, we'll shift focus: **Becoming a Mature Investor** — moving beyond beginners' mistakes into building a sustainable, thoughtful approach for the long run.

Part - V

Becoming a Mature Investor

Chapter - 16
Red Flags to Watch For

Why Red Flags Matter

In unlisted investing, you won't always know the *right* opportunities. But you must learn to recognise the *wrong* ones. Spotting danger early is like a seatbelt — it won't make you rich, but it will save you from ruin.

Remember: **it's better to miss a good deal than to fall into a bad one.**

Red Flag #1: Overhyped Valuations

If a company is being sold at sky-high multiples without solid revenue or profit, pause.

💡 **Example:** During the peak of edtech hype, startups with little profitability sold shares at 50–100x revenue. Later, those valuations collapsed.

Signal to Watch: If brokers keep emphasising "future potential" but can't show current financial strength, it's a bubble.

Red Flag #2: "Guaranteed IPO" Promises

No one — not brokers, not even founders — can guarantee an IPO. Market conditions, regulators, and company performance all play a role.

💡 **Case:** Many Paytm pre-IPO buyers were assured "guaranteed listing gains." Instead, they saw losses.

Signal to Watch: The words *"guaranteed IPO"* or *"sure-shot listing profits."*

Red Flag #3: Lack of Transparency

If the company refuses to share audited financials or basic details, be suspicious.

💡 **Case:** Theranos avoided publishing peer-reviewed data. That secrecy hid fraud for years.

Signal to Watch: Vague answers, delayed documents, or "trust us" responses.

Red Flag #4: Founder Red Flags

Founders are the soul of startups. Red flags include:

- Constantly changing business models.
- Selling too many personal shares early (low skin in the game).
- History of lawsuits or failed ventures.

💡 **Lesson:** Back the jockey (founder), not just the horse (company).

Red Flag #5: Aggressive Brokers

Some brokers push investors with urgency:

"Buy now, limited shares, decision today!"

Pressure selling is a classic scam tactic.

Signal to Watch: Any deal that won't let you think, verify, or compare is a danger zone.

Red Flag #6: Illiquidity without Clarity

Illiquidity is normal in unlisted markets. But if there's no clear plan for exit (IPO, buyback, acquisition), you may be stuck forever.

💡 **Case:** Investors in several mid-sized private companies in India have been waiting over a decade for exits, with no visibility.

Signal to Watch: No exit roadmap, no timeline, just vague "eventually" answers.

Red Flag #7: Complex Structures

If ownership is routed through multiple shell companies, holding companies , or offshore entities, it poses a risk. Complexity often hides debt or legal issues.

Signal to Watch: Diagrams of company ownership that look like a spider's web.

Sidebar: The "Shiny Object" Syndrome

If a company or broker spends more time dazzling you with glossy presentations and less time answering hard questions, beware. Real businesses don't need glitter to prove value.

Red Flag #8: Unrealistic Growth Claims

"We'll grow 10x in one year" sounds exciting, but is rarely realistic. Even giants like Amazon or Reliance grew steadily over decades.

Signal to Watch: Exaggerated projections with no concrete data.

Red Flag #9: No Independent Validation

If all the information you get comes from the seller or broker, danger! Independent sources should confirm the story.

Signal to Watch: No news coverage, no industry reports, no external validation.

Case Study: The ESOP Trap

In 2019, an employee sold ESOPs of a mid-sized startup to a retail investor. The broker claimed "IPO in 18 months." Instead, the company ran out of cash. The shares became worthless.

Lesson: The red flag was visible — there were no audited financials or IPO filings. Excitement blinded the buyer.

The Red Flag Checklist (For Every Deal)

Before buying, ask:

- ✓ Is the valuation supported by numbers, not just hype?
- ✓ Has anyone promised me "guaranteed IPO/listing gains"?

- ✓ Are audited financials available and shared?
- ✓ Do the founders have skin in the game?
- ✓ Am I being pressured to act fast?
- ✓ Is there a clear, realistic exit path?
- ✓ Is the structure simple and transparent?
- ✓ Are growth projections believable?
- ✓ Do I have independent confirmation from at least 2–3 sources?

If more than 2 boxes remain unchecked → walk away.

Closing Thoughts

Red flags don't mean you should never invest. They mean you should pause, investigate, and protect yourself.

Think of red flags as warning signs on a highway. Ignore them, and you risk a crash. Respect them, and you'll navigate safely toward genuine opportunities.

In the next chapter, we'll explore **Networking & Information Sources** — where serious investors actually hang out, and how you can access reliable intelligence in the private market.

Chapter - 17
Networking & Information Sources

Why Networking Matters

In public markets, information is everywhere — news portals, stock tickers, analyst reports. In the unlisted world, it's the opposite: information is scarce, fragmented, and often hidden in private conversations.

That's why **your network is your edge.** The stronger your connections, the better your access to opportunities, data, and wisdom.

As the saying goes:

"In private markets, money follows information. And information follows networks."

Where Serious Investors Hang Out

1. Broker & Platform Networks

Many deals originate from specialised brokers or online platforms. Building relationships here gives you early access.

- Examples (India): UnlistedZone, Planify, SharesCart.
- Examples (Global): EquityZen, Forge Global.

💡 **Tip:** Don't just buy shares — ask questions, build rapport, and learn from how brokers operate.

2. Angel Networks

Formal angel groups bring together investors to co-invest in startups.

- **Examples:** Indian Angel Network (IAN), LetsVenture, AngelList.
- **Pros:** Access to vetted deals.
- **Cons:** Higher minimum investments.

💡 Case: Many Flipkart early backers came from such angel networks.

3. Investor Communities & Forums

Private Telegram, WhatsApp, or LinkedIn groups often circulate deal flow.

- **Pros:** Faster information.
- **Cons:** High risk of rumours and scams — verify everything.

💡 **Rule:** Use these groups for *leads,* not decisions.

4. Startup & Investor Events

Conferences, pitch events, and networking sessions are goldmines for connections.

- **Examples:** TiE Global Summit, Startup Grind, local angel meetups.
- **Benefit:** Meet founders directly, ask hard questions.

5. Personal Networks

Sometimes your colleagues, alumni groups, or family contacts provide access to unlisted opportunities (e.g., employees selling ESOPs).

💡 **Tip:** Treat every contact with respect. One genuine lead can change your investment journey.

Reliable Information Sources

1. Company Filings

- **India:** Ministry of Corporate Affairs (MCA) website, Tofler, ZaubaCorp.
- **Global:** SEC filings (for US firms), Crunchbase, PitchBook.

2. News & Media

Follow startup and business portals:

- **India:** Inc42, YourStory, Economic Times (Startup section).
- **Global:** TechCrunch, CB Insights.

3. Employee Reviews

Sites like Glassdoor or AmbitionBox reveal culture, attrition, and management quality.

4. Industry Reports

Look for sector insights from consulting firms (PwC, EY, Bain). These contextualise whether a company's growth claims are realistic.

The "3-Layer Rule" for Information

Whenever you hear about an opportunity:

1. **Layer 1:** What the broker or seller tells you.
2. **Layer 2:** What independent platforms and filings confirm.
3. **Layer 3:** What your network (experienced investors, insiders) says privately.

Never rely only on Layer 1.

How Beginners Can Start Building Networks

1. **Join 1–2 Platforms** – Sign up, browse available shares, and observe pricing.
2. **Attend 1–2 Events** – Even online webinars help you meet people.
3. **Follow Thought Leaders** – On LinkedIn or Twitter (X), watch how serious investors analyse startups.
4. **Contribute Before Asking** – Share articles, research, or insights in groups. This builds trust.
5. **Build Slowly** – Quality matters more than quantity. A few genuine contacts > hundreds of random forwards.

Case Study: Anjali's Network Effect

Anjali, a young finance professional, began by joining Let'sVenture webinars and following startup news on Inc42. Over a year, she built relationships with two brokers, one angel investor, and an ex-colleague who worked at a unicorn.

- Her first deals came through this network.
- More importantly, she gained access to inside perspectives that no news article could provide.

💡 **Lesson:** Patience in networking creates compounding benefits.

Beginner's Networking Checklist

- Have I joined at least one reputed platform?
- Do I follow at least 5 startup/VC news sources?
- Have I attended one investor event this year?
- Do I know at least one broker personally?
- Do I have 2–3 trusted contacts I can call for advice?

If you can tick these, you're already ahead of most beginners.

Closing Thoughts

Unlisted investing is not a solo journey. Your network is your oxygen. The more reliable your sources, the less likely you are to be misled by hype or scams.

Think of it this way: **money is your fuel, but networks are your map. Without a map, you'll burn through fuel and get nowhere.**

In the next chapter, we'll go deeper into maturity: **Building Your Portfolio Over Time** — how to grow from a few small bets into a structured, balanced portfolio.

Chapter - 18

Building Your Portfolio over Time

Why a Portfolio Approach Matters

Owning one unlisted company is a gamble. Owning several is a strategy. A portfolio turns uncertain bets into a structured plan where winners can cover losers.

In public markets, portfolios protect against volatility. In unlisted markets, they protect against **failure risk.** Since most startups fail, your best defence is spreading smartly and adjusting over time.

The Three Stages of a Beginner's Portfolio

1. Foundation Stage (Year 1–2)

- **Goal:** Learn the process, gain experience.
- **Structure:**
    - 2–3 investments in pre-IPO or mature startups.
    - Small ticket sizes (₹25,000–₹50,000 each).
- **Focus:** Documentation, due diligence, building confidence.

💡 **Example:** Ramesh starts with ₹1.5 lakhs total, spread across NSE pre-IPO shares and an ESOP from Zomato.

2. Expansion Stage (Year 3–5)

- **Goal:** Broaden exposure, take calculated risks.
- **Structure:**
    - 5–7 companies across sectors.
    - Mix of pre-IPO, growth-stage, and 1–2 early-stage startups.
- **Focus:** Diversification, patience, building networks.

💡 **Example:** By Year 4, Ramesh has ₹6 lakhs invested:

- ₹3 lakhs in pre-IPO (safer bets).
- ₹2 lakhs in growth companies.
- ₹1 lakh across two risky early-stage startups.

3. Maturity Stage (Year 6+)

- **Goal:** Balanced portfolio that compounds steadily.
- **Structure:**
    - 8–12 companies.
    - Larger tickets in proven winners.
    - Selective new entries (quality > quantity).
- **Focus:** Exit planning, rebalancing, steady compounding.

💡 **Example:** By Year 8, Ramesh exits NSE shares with strong returns, reinvests into a healthcare startup showing traction, and now has a ₹15 lakh unlisted portfolio.

How to Track Your Portfolio

Unlisted portfolios don't have live tickers. You must build your own system.

1. **Maintain a Spreadsheet** – Record entry price, valuation, and exit plan.
2. **Track Company News** – Set Google Alerts for each firm.
3. **Review Annually** – Once a year, re-check valuations, exit opportunities, and risks.
4. **Stay Patient** – Don't panic if nothing moves for years.

Sidebar: The "Farmer's Calendar"

Think of your portfolio like farming:

- Some crops (companies) sprout quickly.
- Others take years.
- Some die despite care.

Your job is to plant regularly, nurture patiently, and harvest wisely.

The Rebalancing Rule

Every few years, rebalance:

- **Cut exposure** to stagnating companies with no exit path.
- **Double down** on winners showing real traction.
- **Add new seeds** in promising sectors.

💡 **Tip:** Never fall in love with one stock. Love your portfolio, not any single company.

Case Study: Meera's Journey

- **Year 1:** Invested ₹1 lakh across 2 pre-IPO firms.
- **Year 3:** Expanded to 5 companies, ₹5 lakhs total.
- **Year 7:** Exited one winner at 5x returns, reinvested into 2 new growth startups.
- **Year 10:** Portfolio worth ₹20 lakhs, despite 3 total failures.

Lesson: A structured portfolio absorbs failures and rewards patience.

Beginner's Portfolio Checklist

- Do I have at least 3–5 companies in different sectors?
- Is there no single company more than 30% of my unlisted portfolio?
- Have I documented my entry price, exit plan, and lock-in details?
- Do I review once a year and rebalance?
- Am I building steadily, not rushing?

If yes, you're building like a pro.

Closing Thoughts

Building an unlisted portfolio is not about chasing jackpots. It's about steady planting, disciplined care, and patient harvesting. Over the years, this approach transforms scattered bets into a wealth-creating machine.

In the next chapter, we'll look ahead to the **Future of Unlisted Investing** — how technology, regulation, and globalisation are changing the game for tomorrow's investors.

Chapter - 19

The Future of Unlisted Investing

Looking Beyond Today

So far, we've explored the current world of unlisted stocks — its risks, rewards, and mechanics. But the market is evolving. Technology is breaking barriers, regulations are shifting, and access is widening.

For today's beginner, this is exciting news. The private market of tomorrow may look very different from the opaque, network-driven world of today.

Trend #1: Democratisation Through Technology

Until recently, unlisted investing was limited to wealthy insiders. But digital platforms are changing that.

- **Fractional Ownership:** Platforms now allow investors to buy fractions of a share, lowering ticket sizes from lakhs to thousands.
- **Mobile Access:** Apps make it as easy to browse unlisted shares as ordering food.
- **Global Reach:** Platforms connect investors with companies abroad.

💡 **Example:** US platforms like EquityZen let small investors own slices of giants like SpaceX or Stripe before IPOs.

Trend #2: Tokenisation of Equity

Blockchain technology allows shares to be "tokenised"—converted into digital tokens that can be traded securely, instantly, and globally.

- **Pros:** Liquidity improves, transfers become faster, and ownership records are transparent.
- **Cons:** Still experimental, regulatory approval varies across countries.

💡 Imagine buying and selling startup shares on a blockchain exchange, just like crypto trading — with clear ownership trails.

Trend #3: Globalisation of Private Markets

Borders are fading in finance. An Indian investor can back a US startup. A Singaporean investor can buy into an Indian unicorn.

- **Pros:** Diversification across geographies.
- **Cons:** Currency risks, tax complications, and regulatory differences.

💡 **Case:** Many Indian HNIs already own stakes in Silicon Valley startups via global syndicates. Tomorrow, retail investors may too.

Trend #4: Regulatory Evolution

Regulators worldwide are catching up with private markets. Expect:

- Stricter disclosures for large unlisted firms.
- Protection mechanisms for retail investors.
- Tax clarity on unlisted gains.

💡 **Example:** In India, SEBI has already tightened rules for pre-IPO lock-ins and disclosures.

Sidebar: Will Unlisted Become "Listed-Like"?

As private markets grow, they may start to resemble public markets — with transparency, reporting, and even trading platforms. The line between listed and unlisted may blur.

Trend #5: Rise of Alternative Investment Funds (AIFs) and Syndicates

Instead of individuals buying directly, many will pool money into funds that specialise in unlisted shares. This reduces risk through professional management and diversification.

💡 **Example:** AngelList syndicates already allow investors to back curated startup portfolios globally.

What This Means for Beginners

- **Lower Barriers:** Entry amounts will shrink, making it easier to start small.
- **More Liquidity:** Secondary markets and tokenisation may shorten wait times.
- **More Transparency:** Regulations and platforms will reduce fraud risk.

- **More Competition:** As access widens, finding "hidden gems" may become harder.

The Big Picture

The future of unlisted investing is bright, but also competitive. The game is shifting from *who can access* opportunities to *who can analyse and hold patiently.*

Those who develop strong fundamentals — valuation skills, due diligence habits, and emotional discipline — will thrive in this new era.

Beginner's Reflection Exercise

Ask yourself:

- How can I use technology to widen my access?
- Am I prepared to navigate global opportunities?
- How will I keep learning as regulations and tools evolve?

Your answers will guide your future journey.

Closing Thoughts

The private market is no longer a closed club. Tomorrow, it may be as common as mutual funds or listed equities. But remember: while access may become easier, wisdom will always remain rare.

The mature investor is not the one who finds the flashiest platform — it's the one who uses timeless principles in a changing world.

In the final chapter, we'll bring everything together in **Conclusion: The Patient Investor** — a recap of lessons and a mindset reset for your long-term journey.

Chapter - 20
The Patient Investor

Looking Back

We began this journey with a simple idea: unlisted investing is both an opportunity and a trap. Along the way, we've explored:

- What unlisted stocks are and how they work.
- The psychology that drives investors toward dreams and dangers.
- The risks and realities of illiquidity, hype, and fraud.
- The mechanics: finding shares, valuing companies, doing due diligence, and navigating legalities.
- The strategies: starting small, diversifying, planning exits.
- The maturity tools: spotting red flags, building networks, constructing a portfolio, and adapting to the future.

If you've made it here, you're no longer a casual aspirant. You're a learner ready to step into the private markets with clarity and caution.

The Core Message

This book has repeated one theme in many forms: **patience and discipline are your greatest weapons.**

- **Patience** to wait years for exits.
- **Discipline** to resist hype and stick to your rules.
- **Wisdom** to know when to walk away.

Unlisted investing is not about quick jackpots. It is about planting seeds today and waiting for them to grow into forests tomorrow.

The Journey Ahead

You may now be asking: *Where do I go from here?*

Here's a practical roadmap:

1. **Start Small** – Make your first safe, modest investment (₹25k–₹50k).
2. **Build Confidence** – Learn the process of documentation, Demat transfer, and tracking.
3. **Expand Gradually** – Add more companies, diversify across sectors and stages.
4. **Document Everything** – Keep your own records of prices, exits, and learnings.
5. **Review Annually** – Adjust portfolio, rebalance, and reflect.
6. **Stay Patient** – Remember, this is a marathon, not a sprint.

The Investor's Compass

Whenever you feel lost, return to these 5 questions:

1. Can I afford to lose this money if things go wrong?
2. Do I understand how this company actually makes money?
3. Is the price reasonable compared to peers?
4. Am I okay waiting 5–10 years if needed?
5. Do I have a clear exit strategy?

If you can answer "yes" to all five, you are on the right path.

The Bamboo Reminder

Like the Chinese bamboo tree that grows unseen for five years before shooting up 90 feet in six weeks, unlisted investments often test your patience. Your job is to keep watering. Growth will come — not when you want it, but when the time is right.

The Mature Investor's Attitude

The most successful investors share three traits:

- **Humility** – They know they don't know everything.
- **Curiosity** – They keep learning, reading, and asking questions.
- **Resilience** – They accept failures as part of the game.

This is what makes them stand apart from the impatient crowd chasing quick riches.

Closing Words

Unlisted investing is not for everyone. It demands courage, patience, and a long-term view. But for those who stay the course, it offers not just financial rewards but the satisfaction of being part of companies before they become giants.

As you close this book and step into your own journey, remember:

- Start small.
- Diversify wisely.
- Guard against hype.
- Value patience above all.

The jungle of unlisted stocks is vast, full of hidden dangers and treasures. With the lessons here, you are no longer wandering blindly. You carry a map, a compass, and the mind-set of a patient investor.

The rest of the journey is yours. Walk steadily. Water the bamboo. And let time do its quiet magic.

Epilogue - The Journey Continues

As you turn the last page of this book, remember: your journey as an investor is only just beginning.

The private market is vast, unpredictable, and constantly changing. New start-ups will rise, some will stumble, regulations will evolve, and technology will open doors we can only imagine today. What will not change, however, are the timeless principles you now carry: patience, discipline, and clarity.

This book was never meant to give you shortcuts or guarantees. It was meant to be your compass — to point you in the right direction, to remind you when to pause, and to keep you steady when excitement or fear tries to shake you.

You will make mistakes. Every investor does. But if you start small, learn continuously, diversify wisely, and protect yourself with discipline, those mistakes will be small lessons, not devastating losses. And the wins — even if they take years — will reward your patience many times over.

Keep revisiting these chapters when you feel doubt creeping in. Use the checklists, reflect on the stories, and remind yourself of the bamboo tree lesson: growth may be invisible for years before it explodes into view.

The jungle of unlisted stocks is not easy to navigate. But with the right mindset, tools, and patience, it can become not just an investment strategy, but a journey of wisdom and wealth.

Your future as a patient investor is waiting. Step forward with courage, and let time do its quiet, magical work.

📚 Glossary of Key Terms In Unlisted Investing

Term	Definition
Unlisted Stocks	Shares of companies are not traded on stock exchanges such as the NSE or the BSE. Ownership is private, and transactions happen through intermediaries.
Private Equity (PE)	Investments made by institutions or wealthy individuals into mature, unlisted companies for growth or restructuring.
Venture Capital (VC)	Funding is provided to startups or early-stage companies with high growth potential.
Angel Investor	An individual who invests personal funds in startups, usually in exchange for equity.
Pre-IPO	A company that is preparing to go public but has not yet listed its shares on a stock exchange.

ESOP (Employee Stock Ownership Plan)	A company initiative that gives employees partial ownership through shares, aligning their interests with the company's growth.
Secondary Sale	Buying or selling shares from an existing shareholder rather than directly from the company. Common in unlisted markets.
Term Sheet	A preliminary agreement summarises the key terms of an investment before the final contract is signed.
SHA (Shareholders' Agreement)	A legal agreement outlining the rights, duties, and obligations of a company's shareholders.
Due Diligence	Comprehensive research of a company's financials, management, and legal compliance before investing.
Valuation	The process of estimating a company's worth based on assets, profits, growth, or market comparables.
Book Value	The net value of a company's assets minus liabilities, divided by total shares outstanding.
Market Capitalization	The total value of a company's shares in circulation (share price × total shares).

P/E Ratio (Price-to-Earnings)	Indicates how much investors are willing to pay for one unit of the company's earnings.
Liquidity	How easily an asset can be converted into cash without significantly affecting its value.
Lock-in Period	A duration during which shares cannot be sold after investment or IPO.
Exit Strategy	Planned method to liquidate or sell holdings for profit, e.g., IPO, buyback, or acquisition.
Diversification	Distributing investments across multiple sectors or companies to reduce risk.
AIF (Alternative Investment Fund)	SEBI-regulated investment vehicles pool capital for non-traditional assets like startups or private companies.
Seed Funding	The earliest stage of funding a startup, often from founders or angel investors.
Series A/B/C Funding	Successive funding rounds as startups grow and scale.
Unicorn	A privately held startup valued at over $1 billion.

Down Round	A funding round in which a startup's valuation decreases compared to its previous round.
Cap Table (Capitalisation Table)	A record of a company's ownership structure showing equity percentages for all shareholders.
Demat Account	A digital account for holding securities electronically, including unlisted shares.
Registrar of Companies (ROC)	A government authority that manages company incorporation and compliance filings.
MCA (Ministry of Corporate Affairs)	India's governing body for company regulation and financial compliance.
Tokenization	Digitising real assets (like shares) into blockchain-based tokens for easier transfer or trade.
Regulatory Filings	Official documents that companies must file with SEBI or MCA to maintain compliance.
Discounted Cash Flow (DCF)	A valuation method that projects future cash flows and discounts them to present value.
Promoter Holding	Percentage of shares owned by a company's founders or core management.

Pre-Money Valuation	The company's value before new capital is invested.
Post-Money Valuation	The company's value after new funds are added.

Tip: Revisit this glossary whenever you come across a financial term that feels unfamiliar. Understanding the language of investing is half the journey to becoming an informed investor.

🌐 Recommended Resources & Tools for Unlisted Investors

1. Official Government & Regulatory Portals

- **MCA Portal (www.mca.gov.in):**

  Check company registration, directors, annual filings, and compliance status. Always verify if a company is "Active."

- **SEBI (www.sebi.gov.in):**

  Review circulars and updates related to Alternative Investment Funds (AIFs), angel investing, and private market guidelines.

- **NSDL/CDSL:**

  India's primary depositories. Ensure your unlisted shares are dematerialised and securely held.

2. Private Market Platforms

- **UnlistedZone** – India's leading marketplace for verified unlisted shares. Includes analysis and market trends.
- **Planify** – Offers pre-IPO shares, startup equity, and ESOP buybacks.
- **SharesCart / PMS Bazaar / Stockify** – Alternative platforms for secondary-market transactions.

⚠ *Note:* Always verify transaction legitimacy, pricing trends, and counterparty details before any purchase.

3. Company Data & Valuation Tools

- **Tofler / ZaubaCorp / Tracxn / Crunchbase:**

  Excellent sources for company filings, financial ratios, ownership, and valuation history.

- **PitchBook (for professionals):**

  Global database for private market valuations and funding patterns.

💡 *Use at least two independent databases to cross-verify numbers before investing.*

4. Startup & Angel Networks

- Indian Angel Network (IAN)
- LetsVenture
- TiE Global
- 100X.VC

Join these to understand deal flow, industry trends, and networking opportunities. Attending webinars or investor pitch events sharpens your judgment.

5. Knowledge Platforms

- **Moneycontrol / Mint / The Ken / Finshots:**

  For continuous learning, regulatory updates, and macroeconomic analysis.

- **Investopedia (Global):**

  Great for foundational financial concepts and case studies.

- **YourStory / Inc42:**

  Startup news and funding updates that reveal early-stage opportunities.

- **VCCircle / Entrackr:**

  Professional-grade coverage of private equity and venture capital deals.

6. Recommended Learning Habits

1. Set Google Alerts for your shortlisted companies.
2. Track startup valuation reports quarterly.
3. Maintain an "Investment Journal" — note every decision and its reasoning.
4. Revisit your portfolio every six months to test for bias or drift.

7. Tech Tools for the Smart Investor

- **Google Sheets + API Plugins:** Track unlisted stock metrics and valuations over time.
- **Notion:** Build your own investor dashboard.
- **LinkedIn:** Follow founders and investor groups—often where early whispers about deals begin.

💬 ***Final Thought:***

You don't need to predict the next unicorn — you need to understand why it becomes one. These tools and habits will give you an edge not through luck, but through insight, patience, and preparation.

A Note of Gratitude

I would like to express my heartfelt gratitude to every reader who has chosen to be part of this movement toward informed and patient investing. Your curiosity, discipline, and commitment to continuous learning reflect the true spirit of a wise investor — one who builds wealth with purpose, not impulse.

By seeking knowledge before action, you are contributing to a new generation of financially aware Indians who think about the long term, invest responsibly, and inspire others to do the same. It is my sincere hope that the insights shared in this book empower you to approach investing with confidence, clarity, and calm.

Keep learning, keep growing, and always remember — wealth built on wisdom stands the test of time.

— ***Vinayak Savanur***

Let's Stay Connected

Scan the QR code below to connect with me on **LinkedIn** and join a growing community of thoughtful, long-term investors. Stay updated with my latest insights, articles, and projects focused on unlisted and equity investing. You can also connect directly.

Let's Stay Connected!

www.linkedin.com/in/vinayaksavanur

📓 Also by Vinayak Savanur

India's first presentation-style investing book — simple, powerful, and already changing how people think about equity investing.

The Index Revolution isn't 400 pages of jargon — it's 100 pages of clarity that actually makes sense. Designed for readers who want financial wisdom without the noise, this book makes the art of index-based investing practical, visual, and refreshingly easy to understand.

It's not just a book — it's a **financial literacy movement.**

Be part of it today and see how disciplined, passive investing can reshape your relationship with equity markets.

Available now on:

amazon **Amazon,**

Flipkart **Flipkart, and**

amazonkindle **Kindle**

Don't wait — you'll want to be early in this revolution!